AF413546

PILOT'S
CAREER GUIDE

PILOT'S CAREER GUIDE

Step by Step Learn How to Become an International Airline Pilot

Editors
Capt Shekhar Gupta
Niriha Khajanchi

Notion Press

Old No. 38, New No. 6
McNichols Road, Chetpet
Chennai - 600 031

First Published by Notion Press 2017
Copyright © Shekhar Gupta 2017
All Rights Reserved.

ISBN 978-1-947027-70-1

Foreword

With the education becoming the base of future, choosing a right career option is like laying the foundation block to anyone's life. Traditional options available are easy to pursue for reason you have been hearing a lot about them already and the information related to it are most easily accessible. After all it is not hard to find which college to choose for a Bachelors Degree and a Masters Degree in Commerce, Business Studies, Finance, and Human Resource, what are the requirements for every course and the procedure to get enrolled.

The actual problem comes in taking the road less traveled, Pursuing the Career that is not taken by every third individual, like Dreaming to becoming an Airline Commercial Pilot. Across the world there are thousands of Flying Training Academies providing Commercial Pilot Training to starters but none counseling center to Guide these young aspirants about the immense Paper work like Medical requirement, Theory papers, Conversion papers, different specific requirements for each Pilot Certifications and more.

This book must successfully attempts in throwing light to all the above aspects and most importantly highlights the Job Prospects of Pilots in the industry in countries specifically like, Australia, Philippines, Canada, USA, UK, New Zealand and India.

I am Flying with Jet Airways India Limited as Senior Commander having more than 10000 Hrs of Flying on many different types of Aircrafts. I had the problem when I wanted to become a Pilot. I was the 1st Generation Pilot in my family. No One was there to guide me "How to Become a Pilot"

Captain Pulkit Gupta

Sr. Commander [Boeing 737]

Jet Airways I Ltd

Acknowledgments

From the idea to finally the publishing of Book could not have been possible without all the team members of AeroSoft Corp and the Pilots who are serving the Aviation Industry all Over. Pilot Career Guide is the outcome of all the queries that comes to us on daily basis regarding the career in Aviation Industry and more importantly Pilot training. And so we decided to answer all the questions and give all possible useful information to help you make decision by our book.

We are grateful to all Captains, Captain Simmi Bhullar, Captain Ankisha Awasthi, Captain Yashika Mahajan, Captain Viral Das Delta Airlines USA, Captain Hamza, Captain Pulkit Gupta, Captain Prashant, Captain Monika, Captain Monu Khanna, Captain Rashmi Air India, Captain Manish Thakur of Jet Airways, Captain Sameer Tiwari, Captain Faizal Ali Khan, Captain Divyesh Patel, Captain Paula, Captain Azam Khan, Captain Devi Prasad Shetti Captain Bhaskar Pant of Buddha Air Nepal, Captain Mark Tube, Captain Somesh Bhatnagar, Captain Devi Prasad for making the publication of this book possible.

We deeply thank our team members at AeroSoft Corp and Mission To Canada who believed in us and supported us in all possible means. All Pilots from more than 200 Flight Schools who gave us Information to be shared here. Aruna Sharma, Poonam Sharma, Ankita Paruthi, Ria Shisodia, Seema Chauhan thank you for your dedicated work. We also thank few industry people Poonam Jacob of Indigo, Shital Upare of Singapore Airlines, Komal Soni of Air India, Khushi Damania Cabin Crew Indigo to keep us motivating and constantly keeping us updated about the Airline Industry.

Table of Contents

Introduction

Very few Education Institutes and Traditional Careers like engineering, science graduates, medical And Chartered accountants etc. are the options that still prevail but with growing awareness and knowledge these career options have grown vastly – like Civil Aviation Sector.

Aviation - the very word reminds us of a Pilot dressed in crisp and Smart Pilots Uniform, Flying the big giant Bird with Elegance and Flying Skill.

Pilot Training involves certain number of Flying hours to be completed with Night Landing, Instrument Rating [IR], Pilots Medical Requirements, Multi Engine Rating [MEL] theory papers etc. followed by conversion papers if Flying done outside your own country. All these requirements are not that simple as it looks like, and so we attempt to cater all such necessary information in detail for all the aspirants who wants to have an Aviation Career in the leading Civil Aviation Industry.

This book attempts in answering all general questions that pop ups as soon as one chose to select a Career path like-

Whether Aviation is fit or not?

What are the basic Requirements and Eligibility criteria of becoming an Airline or Corporate Commercial Pilot?

What all courses one needs to study in the course of becoming a Pilot?

Which is the best known Flight Training School or Flying Clubs?

What would be the approx Overall Fee structure and financing facility available? And most importantly, the books enlightens –

- The true picture of the current Pilots Job scenario across the Globe

- The areas other than Airlines that have Pilots Job Opportunities

- Best attempt to get a Pilots Jobs

- Assistance in an Airlines Interview Questions.

About the Editors

Capt Shekhar Gupta

Shekhar is a Professional Pilot with more than 8 years experience of Flying on 14 different types of Aircrafts in 10 different countries with accident free Flying record. Shekhar is good in Flying Training as well as in Ground class for Pilots. Shekhar started his Flying career from Skycabs [Colombo] and worked for many Airlines Training Companies from different part of the world. He trained more than 350 Pilots who are Flying worldwide. He is a member of Aircraft Owners & Pilots Association [USA], Royal Society of Aeronautics [UK], Delhi Flying Club, Aeronautical Society of India, MP Flying Club Indore, Aeronautical Research Society. Before Editing this book Shekhar personally visited more than Top 200 Aviation Academies from more than 15 different countries.

Shekhar is a frequent Flyer on AA, Air India, British Airways, Cathay Pacific, Delta Airlines, Emerites, Ethihad, Jet Airways, Kingfisher and many more. Shekhar is an active member of www.MissionToCanada.com a micro Business Mission set up by Govt. of Canada and Air Transport Association of Canada. His recent passion is Aviation Blogging and Aviation SEO for which he takes classes for IIT & IIM students in India and other Pilots from different countries in abroad. Shekhar is also a Co-Founder of www.AirAviator.com a new Aviation StartUp.

Niriha Khajanchi

Niriha is working with AeroSoft Corp as a Project Manager. Born and brought up in Indore, Madhya Pradesh, She did her MBA in Aviation Management from University of Petroleum and Energy Studies and has completed her Bachelors degree from DAVV, Indore. She has an experience in content writing and has done internship at GMR Aviation Pvt. Ltd., Bangalore. She has 50 Hours of Flying experience on Cessna 152 Aircraft. Niriha is well equipped with the knowledge of various domain specific courses along with basic management subjects like Airport Planning Management, Fundamentals of Airline operations, Aviation Safety and security, Aviation Law and Regulatory management and Customer Relationship Management, Airport and Airline Economics. She is keenly interested in writing notes and journals.

CHAPTER 1
Your Aviation Career Starts Here

Dear Aspirants,

Wishing You a Very Happy Take Off!

Choosing a career option to be pursued requires a lot of research work that includes the future possibility, requirements, duration, and the investment needed. And knowing about all this information is the first step to accomplish since this act as a basis for the decision. The book is a one stop shop for all the young aspirants who wish to make a career in the field.

Becoming an Airline Pilot is one of the fascinating options available; this book helps you to have a clear picture of it.

We have included this section to help and explain the Pilot's opportunities and after that how to get about with their future plans. We have also thought it prudent to include some of the many pitfalls or setbacks that await the financially unwary in what is otherwise a very loving and passionate Profession. Every country has its own Civil Aviation Department who manages Aviation activities. You must make sure here we are talking about only Civil Aviation industry not defense or military Flying. If you want to become a Fighter Pilot than the procedure is very different from that of a commercial Pilot

Before all that, Why should you become a Professional Pilot?

The possible reasons may be

- *Passion*

- *Glamour*

- *Reputation*

- *Career*

- *Born Pilot [Childhood Desire]*

Before you embark, it is most important that you get an assessment from your country's "Civil Aviation Department" about the recognition of the license you are hoping to get and the answers of following general questions like -

Is the License fully recognized by your civil Aviation when you return back home? Also read CAR [Civil Aviation Requirements] thoroughly.

What are the different types of Certificates?

- *PPL Private Pilot License*

- *CPL Commercial Pilot License*

- *IR Instrument Rating*

- *MEL Multi Engine Land [Rating]*

- *CFI Chief Flying Instructor*

- *ATPL Airline Transport Pilot License*

International Pilot Training Industry:

Aviation worldwide is a recurring market and the industry is affected predominantly by economics, politics and some part of the globe with acute terrorism etc. 9/11 had a negative impact on the entire Airline Industry across the globe while in other regions tourism sustained.

Not all Pilots choose an Airline career. There are many others as equally rewarding. Other areas available are crop spraying, Charter Flying, Flying for Air Ambulance or Medical Services etc. Although we don't recommend it if you intend going the Airline route.

Remuneration is one difficult subject to generalize on as salaries vary extensively around the world. Crop spraying is renowned as being a well paid Job but this will be cyclically dependant on the seasons. Internationally, Salary of the Second Officer ranges between USD $ 600 per month to USD $ 1500 per month; First Officer USD $ 1000 per month to USD $ 3500 per month and for a Captain between USD $ 2000 per month to USD $ 8500 per month. The salary depends on the Airline you fly and the number of hours/years of service.

Normally the period of transition from a First Officer to a Captain is 3 to10 Years. Small and developing countries like Nepal, Burma pay less Salaries and Countries like Africa, Canada and UK pay best Salaries in the world. In countries like India some of the Captains of small Charter Airlines gets less then USD $ 1500 per Month.

Few fortunate Pilots become Captain in 2 to 5 years. Pilot salaries have drastically fallen down due to slowdown of economy and industry thriving in various parts of the world.

Due to Global Aviation Recession, Aviation Industry is going through a rough phase. But, with the economy growing consistently and increasing purchasing power of people across the Globe the International Aviation Industry is bound to grow. The importance of time over money is a key to making a transition from the railways to Airlines as a primary mode of transport.

Flying however is a universal skill and once you have a few thousand hours under the belt, the world is open with opportunities.

Take off is optional but landing is compulsory.

Best Of Luck!

Shekhar Gupta

Niriha Khajanchi

CHAPTER 2
Flight Training

[PILOT TRAINING]

1. Pilot Training involves Mechanical Pilot's skill along with operational knowledge and understanding of the associated elements essential in Flying. This Training ensures the most important factor of Aviation as an industry – that is Safety.

2. The basic concept in Flight Training starts from understanding of – "Theory of Flight" that is actually Principles of Flying. Now how skillfully a Pilot applies those Principles in performing maneuvers makes him/her a good and Safe Pilot. Ground instruction and Pre Flight Training go hand in hand. Together both Trainings are meaningful and comprehensive.

3. The Primary purpose of all Flight Training is to develop Safe and Proficient Pilots. The student Pilot must be cooperative in attaining these objectives. Flight Briefing and De Briefing with Pilot Instructor is very important.

4. Every Aviation Regulator lists the requirements that are required to be met before a person is Certified as any Pilot. These requirements include applicant's eligibility criteria as age, health, Physical condition, mental condition, Aeronautical Experience, fluent English, General knowledge, and clear communication skill. It also mentions the subject of Aeronautical Knowledge that the applicant Pilot should be thorough with for any certifications.

5. To function as a Pilot in Command of a Flight one needs to be skilled in maneuvers and knowledge to cater safe and efficient Flight.

Trainer Aircrafts

1. As clear from the nomenclature, Trainer Aircrafts is the different class Aircraft that are designed specifically to facilitate Training of Pilots and Aircrews. These Aircrafts have additional safety features—such as Solo Flight controls and simplified Cockpit arrangement allowing the trainee Pilots to safely advance their real-time Piloting, Civilian Pilots are given Training in light Aircraft usually with two seats, one for instructor and another for the trainee. One of the common configurations is termed as Tandem that is side by side seating arrangement inside the cockpit. This allows the communication and whole learning process go smoothly.

2. While in case of Military Flight Training it is usually in phases so that each phase they eliminate the unsuitable candidates as the Training expenses are too high. The phases are-

3. Ab-initio (where Pilot Training is given in Light Aircrafts)

4. Basic Pilot Training

5. Advanced Pilot Training

6. Operational Conversions

7. Multi Engine Flight Trainers

8. Navigation Trainers

Chapter 3
Pilots License

[FLIGHT RATINGS]

In India

DGCA, Directorate General Civil Aviation, is the Indian regulatory body that states the requirements for different Certifications in Aviation. The types of Pilot's Licenses given are –

SPL – Student Pilot License

PPL – Private Pilot License

CPL – Commercial Pilot License

ATPL – Airline Transport Pilot License

IR – Instrument Rating

FRTOL – Flight Radio Telephone Operator License

As per Indian DGCA, following guidelines have been mentioned –

1. **SPL [Student Pilot's License is issued for Airplanes, Helicopters or Gliders]**

   a. Requirements -
      * Age — The applicant should be minimum 16 years of age.
      * Educational Qualification — He should have passed Class Ten or its equivalent examination from a recognized Board.

- Medical fitness — She/he should produce on a prescribed Performa a certificate of physical fitness from an approved medical practitioner after undergoing a medical examination as per the requirements notified by the Director-General.

- Knowledge — She/he should pass oral examination in Air Regulations, Air Navigation, Aviation Meteorology and Aircraft and Engines, unless he previously held a Pilot's license of a higher category.

b. Validity -

The period of validity commences from the date of issue or renewal of the license. For Student Pilot's License the validity is for 5 years and Validity of medical fitness assessment 24 months.

c. Renewal—

The license has to be renewed before the validity gets expired.

d. Aircraft Rating—

The license should indicate the class and the types of Aircraft the holder is entitled to fly.

e. Privileges-

The privileges of the holder of a Student Pilot's License should be to fly within Indian Territory only, as Pilot-in-Command of any Airplane, Helicopter or Glider entered in the Aircraft rating of his license Provided that:-

- She/he should fly at all times under the authority and supervision of a Flight Instructor or an Approved Examiner;

- She/he should fly an Aircraft under Visual Flight Rules only;

- She/he should not carry passengers, animals and goods or fly for hire, reward or remuneration of any kind;

- She/he should not undertake cross-country Flights unless he has a minimum of ten hours of solo Flight time and has passed the examinations in Air Navigation and Aviation Meteorology.

2. **PPL [Private Pilot's License (Aeroplanes)]**

a. Requirements —

- Age — He should not be less than 17 years of age on the date of application.

- Educational Qualification — He should have passed Class Ten or equivalent Examination from a recognized Board.

- Medical Fitness — He should produce on a prescribed proforma, a certificate of physical fitness from an approved medical practitioner after undergoing a medical examination.

- Knowledge — He/She should pass a written examination in Air Regulations, Air Navigation, Aviation Meteorology and Aircraft and Engines as per the syllabus prescribed by the Director-General. An applicant in possession of a valid Private Pilot's License (Helicopters) or a Commercial/ Airline Transport Pilot's License (Helicopters) should pass an examination in Aircraft and Engines only.

- Experience — He/She should produce evidence of having satisfactorily completed as a Pilot of an aeroplane for minimum 40 hours of Flight time which should include—

- minimum 20 hours of solo Flight time;

- minimum 5 hours of cross-country Flight time as the sole occupant of an aeroplane including a Flight of minimum 150 nautical miles in the course of which full stop landings at two different aerodromes should have been made;

- minimum 10 hours of solo Flight time completed within a period of 12 months immediately preceding the date of application for the issue of license;

- Skill— He should have perform as a Pilot-in-command or a Co-Pilot of an airplane, to the satisfaction of an Examiner, on the type of airplane to which the application for the license relates, within a period of 6 months immediately preceding the date of application.

b. Validity –

The period of validity commences from the date of issue or renewal of the license. For Private Pilot's License the validity is for 10 years and Validity of medical fitness assessment is 24 months.

c. Renewal –

The license may be renewed on receipt of satisfactory evidence of the applicant —

- having undergone a medical examination;

- having satisfactorily minimum 5 hours of Flight time as Pilot-in-command of an Aeroplane within a period of 12 months immediately

d. Ratings -

- Aircraft Rating—

The license should indicate the class and the types of Airplane the holder is entitled to fly. An open rating for all single piston engine types of Airplane having an all up weight not exceeding 1500kgs. may also be granted if he has completed minimum 250 hours as Pilot-in-command and has at least four different types of Aeroplane entered in the Aircraft rating of his license Provided that the privileges of the open rating should be exercised only after having undergone a ground and Flight familiarization with a Flight Instructor for the type of Aircraft and a certificate should be recorded by the Flight Instructor/Examiner in the Pilot's Log book.

- Night Rating— Night Rating entitles the holder of the license to carry passengers at night.

Conditions for the issue of this Rating are:-

- ▷ He/She must have completed minimum 50 hours of Flight time as Pilot-in -command and as sole manipulator of the controls including minimum 5 hours by night, which must include a minimum of 5 take-offs and 5 landings.

> He/She must have completed a dual cross-country Flight by night of at least 100 nautical miles before he can be permitted to undertake sole cross-country Flights by night, and

> He/She must have completed minimum 5 hours of dual instructions in instrument Flying which may include not less than two and a half hours on an approved synthetic Flight trainer.

- Instrument Rating— Instrument rating entitles the holder of the license to fly under the Instrument Flight Rules.

e. Extension of Aircraft Rating—

For extension of Aircraft Rating to include an additional type of aeroplane, an applicant should be required to produce evidence of —

- He/She must passed written examination in Aircraft and Engines;

- He/she must undergo adequate dual instructions and solo Flying on the type;

- He/she must satisfactorily complete the Flight test on the type within a period of 6 months immediately preceding date of application for the extension of Aircraft Rating.

f. Privileges—

The privileges of the holder of a Private Pilot's License should be to act as Pilot-in-command or as Co-Pilot of any Aeroplane which is entered in the Aircraft Rating of his/her license and carry passengers therein:

Provided that —

- No Flight is undertaken for hire or remuneration of any kind;

- The passengers are carried by night only when the holder of license has a valid night rating;

- No Flight should be undertaken under the Instrument Flight Rules without having a valid Instrument Rating.

3. CPL [Commercial Pilot's License (Aeroplanes)]

  a. Requirements -

- Age -

  He/She should not be less than 18 years on the date of application.

- Educational Qualification –

  He/She should have passed Class Ten plus Two or an equivalent examination with Physics and Mathematics, from a recognized Board/University.

- Medical Fitness—

  He/She should produce on a prescribed Performa a certificate of physical fitness from an approved Medical Board after undergoing a medical Examination as per the requirements as notified by the Director-General under Rule 39B.

- Knowledge —

  He/She should pass a written examination in Air Regulations, Air Navigation Meteorology and Aircraft and Engines and Signals (practical) examination for interpretation of aural and visual signals, as per the syllabus prescribed by the Director-General:

- Experience— He/She shall produce evidence of having completed as a Pilot of an aeroplane within 5 years immediately preceding the date of application for license not less than two hundred hours of Flight time, which shall include—

- Minimum 100 hours of Flight time as Pilot-in-Command of which not less than fifteen hours shall have been completed within a period of six months immediately preceding the date of application for license;

- Not less than twenty hours of cross-country Flight time as Pilot-in-Command including a cross-country Flight of not less than three hundred nautical miles in the course of which full stop landings at two different aerodromes shall be made;

- Not less than ten hours of instrument time of which not more than five hours may be on an approved simulator; and

- Not less than five hours of Flight time by night including a minimum of ten take-offs and ten landings as Pilot-in-Command as (sole manipulator of controls) carried out within six months immediately proceedings the date of application for license.

- Flying Training— He/She shall have completed the Flying Training in accordance with the syllabus prescribed by the Director-General.

- Other Requirements— He/She shall be in possession of a current Flight Radio Telephone Operator's License for operation of radio telephone apparatus on board an Aircraft issued by the Director-General.

- Skill— He/She shall have demonstrated his competency to perform the procedures and maneuvers prescribed in the syllabus to the satisfaction of an examiner, on the type of Aeroplane to which the application for license relates, within a period of six months immediately preceding the date of application. The competency shall be demonstrated in —

- General Flying Test by day [GFT – Day]

- General Flying Test by Night; [GFT Night]

- A cross-country Flight test by day consisting of a Flight of not less than two hundred fifty nautical miles in the course of which at least one full stop landing at an aerodrome other than the aerodrome of departure shall be made; and

- A cross-country Flying test by night consisting of a Flight of not less than one hundred twenty nautical miles returning to the place of departure without landing elsewhere.

b. Validity—

The period of validity shall commence from the date of issue or renewal of the license. Validity of license - 5 Years and Validity of medical fitness assessment - 12 Months

c. Renewal—

The license may be renewed on receipt of evidence of the applicant —

- Having undergone a medical examination in accordance with para 1(c) above;

- Having satisfactorily completed not less than 10 hours of Flight time as Pilot-in-Command within a period of six months immediately preceding the date of application for renewal; or in lieu thereof, having satisfactorily completed the general Flying test by day and night as laid down in clause (h) of paragraph 1 within the same period;

- Having a current Flight Radio Telephone Operator's License for operation of radio telephone apparatus on board an Aircraft, issued by the Director-General.

d. Aircraft Rating—

- The license shall indicate the types of aeroplane the holder is entitled to fly.

- An open rating for all single piston engine type of aeroplane having an all up weight not exceeding 1500kgs may also be granted if he has completed not less than one thousand hours of Flight time on such types of aeroplane including not less than five hundred hours as Pilot-in-Command and has at least four different types of Aircraft entered in the Aircraft rating of his license:

  ▷ Provided that the privileges of the open rating shall be exercised only after having undergone a ground and Flight familiarization with a Flight Instructor or an approved.

  ▷ Examiner and a certificate to this effect shall be recorded by the Examiner in the Pilot's log book, before the Pilot is released to exercise the privileges of open rating on that type of Aircraft.

- Instructor's Rating –

Instructor's Rating entitles the holder to impart Flying instructions.

- Instrument Rating –

Instrument Rating entitles the holder to fly under Instrument Flight Rules.

- Flying Training—

  He should have completed the Flying Training in accordance with the syllabus prescribed by the Director-General.

- Other Requirements—

  He/she shall be in possession of a current Flight Radio Telephone Operator's License for operation of radio telephone apparatus on board an Aircraft issued by the Director-General.

- Skill—

  He shall have demonstrated his performance the procedures and maneuvers prescribed in the syllabus to the satisfaction of an examiner, on the type of aeroplane to which the application for license relates, within a period of six months immediately preceding the date of application. The competency shall be demonstrated as in —

  ▷ General Flying test by day;

  ▷ General Flying test by night;

  ▷ A cross-country Flight test by day consisting of a Flight of not less than 250 nautical miles in the course of which at least one full stop landing at an aerodrome other than the aerodrome of departure shall be made; and

  ▷ A cross-country Flying test by night consisting of a Flight of not less than 120 nautical miles returning to the place of departure without landing elsewhere.

e. Extension of Aircraft Rating—

  An applicant shall be required to produce evidence of –

  (i) having passed a written examination in Aircraft and Engines as mentioned in para 1(d) and of having gained, under appropriate supervision, experience in Flying the Aircraft of such type or on approved Flight simulator in respect of the following, namely:-

- Normal Flight procedures and maneuvers during all phases of Flight;

- Abnormal and emergency procedures and maneuvers in the event of failures and malfunctions of equipment, such as power plant, systems and airframe;

- where applicable, instrument procedures, including instrument approach, missed approach and landing procedures under normal, abnormal and emergency conditions, including simulated engine failure;

- Procedures for crew incapacitation and crew coordination including allocation of Pilot tasks crew cooperation and use of check lists; and

  ▷ Having satisfactorily completed the general Flying tests by day and night in accordance with para 1(h) in respect of the type of Aircraft for which the extension of Aircraft rating is desired. Such Flying tests shall have been completed within a period of six months immediately preceding the date of the application for extension of the Aircraft rating.

f. Privileges—

The privileges of the holder of a Commercial Pilot's License shall be:—

- To exercise all the privileges of Private Pilot's License;

- To act as Pilot-in-Command of any aeroplane having an all-up-weight not exceeding 5700kg and which is entered in the Aircraft rating of his license provided that when passengers are to be carried at night, he shall have carried out within a period of six months immediately preceding the date of the intended Flight not less than ten take-offs and ten landings by night as Pilot-in-Command:

- To act as Co-Pilot of any aeroplane where a Co-Pilot is required to be carried and which is entered in the Aircraft rating of his license:

Provided that for all Flights under the Instrument Flight Rules, either as Pilot-in- Command or as Co-Pilot, he shall have a current Instrument Rating: Provided further that for all Flights as Co-Pilot of transport Airplane having an all-up weight exceeding 5700kgs he shall have carried out within the preceding six months of the intended Flight, appropriate proficiency checks in respect of that type of Aircraft as required by the Director-General.

4. ATPL [Airline Transport Pilot's License (Aeroplanes)]

a. Requirements—

- Age — Minimum 21 years of age.

- Educational Qualification — He shall have passed class ten plus two with Physics and mathematics or its equivalent examination from a recognized Board/University.

- Medical Fitness — He shall produce on a prescribed Performa a certificate of physical fitness from an approved Medical Board after undergoing a medical examination, during which he shall have established his medical fitness on the basis of compliance with the requirements as notified by the Director-General under Rule 39B;

- Knowledge — He shall pass a written and oral examination in Air Regulations, Air Navigation, Avionics (Radio Aids and Instruments), Aviation Meteorology and Aircraft and Engines, and Signals (Practical) examination for interpretation of aural and visual signals as per the syllabus prescribed by the Director-General.

- Experience — He shall produce evidence of having satisfactorily completed as a Pilot of an aeroplane not less than 1500 hours of Flight time of which not less than 150 hours Flight time shall be in the preceding twelve months and his total Flying experience shall include —

  ▷ not less than 500 hours of Flight time as Pilot-in-Command or as Co-Pilot performing, under the supervision of a Pilot who fulfills the Flying experience requirements of a check Pilot, the duties and functions of a Pilot-in-command provided that at least two hundred hours out of these shall be cross-country Flight time, including not less than fifty hours of Flight time by night.

  ▷ Not less than one thousand hours of total cross-country Flight time;

- ▷ Not less than one hundred hours of Flight time by night;

- ▷ Not less than one hundred hours of instrument time under actual or simulated instrument conditions of which not less than fifty hours shall be in actual Flight;

- ▷ Not less than ten hours of Flight time completed within a period of six months immediately preceding the date of application for the license.

- Other Requirements—

  - ▷ He shall be the holder of a Commercial or a Senior CPL. However, this will not be applicable for the issue of ATPL to a Pilot from Armed Forces who otherwise meets the requirements;

  - ▷ He shall have a current Instrument Rating;

  - ▷ He shall be in possession of a current Flight Radio Telephone Operator's License.

- Skill—

  He shall have demonstrated his competency to perform by day and by night the procedures and maneuvers prescribed in the syllabus to the satisfaction of the Examiner, on the type of multi-engine aeroplane to which the application for license relates within a period of six months immediately preceding the date of application.

b. Validity—

Validity of medical fitness assessment - 12 Months

Validity of License - 2 years.

c. Renewal—

The License may be renewed on receipt of satisfactory evidence of the applicant —

- Having undergone a medical examination in accordance with para 1(c).

- Having satisfactorily completed not less than ten hours Flight time as Pilot-in-Command (fifty percent of Flight

time as Co-Pilot may be counted towards the requirements of Flight time as Pilot-in-Command) within a period of six months immediately preceding the date of application for renewal, or in lieu thereof; having satisfactorily completed the Flying tests by day and by night as laid down in clause (g) of paragraph 1 within the same period.

- Having a current Flight Radio Telephone Operator's License.

- Having satisfactorily completed Instrument Rating Flight Test on a multiengine aeroplane entered in the License within the preceding twelve months of the date of intended Flight.

d. Ratings—

- Aircraft Rating—

   The license shall indicate the class and the types of Airplane the holder is entitled to fly. An open rating for all types of Airplane having all-up-weight not exceeding 5700kgs may also be granted if he has completed not less than 1000 hours of Flight time as a Pilot-in-Command on any aeroplane having an all-up-weight of 14,000kgs or above.

- Instructor's Rating—

   Instructor's Rating entitles the holder to impart Flying instructions.

- Instrument Rating—

   No separate instrument rating is provided for in the license. The privileges of instrument rating are included in the privileges of this license provided that the instrument rating Flight tests have been carried out to the satisfaction of the Director-General within a period of twelve months immediately preceding the intended Flight under Instrument Flight Rules.

e. Extension of Aircraft Rating—

For extension of Aircraft rating to include an additional type of aeroplane, an applicant shall be required to produce evidence of (i) having passed a written examination in Aircraft and

Engines as mentioned in para 1(d) and of having gained, experience in Flying the Aircraft of such type or on approved Flight simulator in respect of the following.

- Normal Flight procedures and maneuvers during all phases of Flight;

- Abnormal and emergency procedures and maneuvers in the event of failures and malfunctions of equipment, such as power plant, systems and airframe;

- where applicable, instrument procedures, including instrument approach, missed approach and landing procedures under normal, abnormal and emergency conditions, including simulated engine failure;

- procedures for crew incapacitation and crew coordination including allocation of Pilot tasks, crew cooperation and use of check lists; and (ii) having satisfactorily completed the general Flying tests by day and night in accordance with para 1(h) in respect of the type of Aircraft for which the extension of Aircraft rating is desired. Such Flying tests shall have been completed within a period of six months immediately preceding the date of the application for extension of the Aircraft rating.

f. Privileges—

The privileges of the holder of an Airline Transport Pilot's License shall be:—

- To exercise the privileges of a private, a Commercial and a Senior Commercial Pilot's License;

- To act as Pilot-in-Command or as Co-Pilot of any aeroplane where a Co-Pilot is required to be carried and which is entered in the Aircraft rating of his license:

Provided that he shall not act as Pilot-in-Command of an aeroplane having a all-up-weight exceeding 5700kgs unless he has completed on that type of aeroplane not less than one hundred hours of Flight time as a Co-Pilot, followed by ten consecutive satisfactory route checks of which

not less than five shall be by night under the supervision of a Check Pilot, performing the duties and functions of a Pilot-in-command and has demonstrated his competency to fly as a Pilot-in-Command to the satisfaction of the Director General Provided further that for all Flights as Pilot-in-Command or as Co-Pilot on transport Airplane having an all-up-weight exceeding 5700kgs, he shall have undergone satisfactorily within the preceding six months of the intended Flight, appropriate proficiency checks in respect of that type of Aircraft as required by the Director-General. Provided also that for all IFR Flights as Pilot-in-Command or as Co-Pilot, he shall be required to have current Instrument Rating.

5. Instrument Rating (IR) [Aeroplanes]

a. Requirements —

- Knowledge— He/She shall pass a written and oral examination in Air Regulations, Air Navigation, Aviation Meteorology and Instrument Rating as per syllabus prescribed by the Director-General for issue of Commercial Pilot's License. He shall also pass a practical test on interpretation of aural and visual signals as per the syllabus prescribed by the Director-General.

- Experience—

  He/She shall produce evidence of having satisfactorily completed as a Pilot of an aeroplane—

  ▷ Not less than one hundred hours of Flight time as a Pilot-in-Command including not less than fifty hours of cross-country Flight time;

  ▷ Not less than forty hours of instrument time of which not more than twenty hours shall be instrument ground time. A minimum of five hours of instrument time shall have been completed within a period of six months immediately preceding the date of application for the Instrument Rating:

- Other Requirements —

  He shall be:

  ▷ Holder of a current Pilot's License (Aeroplanes);

  ▷ Holder of a current Flight Radio Telephone Operator's License.

- Flying Training— He/She shall have completed the Flying Training in accordance with the syllabus as prescribed by the Director-General.

- Skill— He/She shall have demonstrated to the satisfaction of the Examiner his competency to fly an aeroplane in respect of which Instrument Rating is desired, solely with the aid of instruments by undergoing an instrument Flying test within a period of six months immediately preceding the date of application for the rating. The Flying test shall be carried out in accordance with the syllabus as prescribed by the Director-General.

b. Validity—

The rating shall be valid for a period of twelve months from the date of the satisfactory completion of the instrument rating test.

c. Renewal—

The Instrument Rating may be renewed on receipt of satisfactory evidence of the applicant:

- Having satisfactorily completed the Instrument Rating Flight Test as laid down in para 1(e).

- Having a valid Flight Radio Telephone Operator's License issued by the Director-General.

d. Extension of Instrument Rating—

For extension an applicant shall be required to produce evidence of having satisfactorily completed the Flight test in accordance with para 1(e) in respect of the type of aeroplane for which the extension of Instrument Rating is desired. The Flight test shall have been completed within a period of six months immediately preceding the date of application for the extension of Instrument Rating.

e. Privileges—

The privileges of the holder thereof shall be to fly under the Instrument Flight Rules, the types of Airplane on which he has demonstrated his competency in accordance with para 1(e).

In Canada

TC- **Transport Canada** is responsible for licensing Pilots and other aviation specialists (such as dispatchers and mechanics) as well as registering and inspecting Aircraft. It is also responsible for the safety certification and continuous safety oversight of most forms of commercial operations.

The skill requirements for the issuance of different licenses as per TC are as follows:

Private Pilot License PPL-

Private Pilot License of Aeroplane's requirements is clearly set out in the Flight test guide as per the Transport Canada. Flight Instructors must use this guide to prepare the applicants for Flight tests. Every applicant should be familiar with this guide and refer to the qualification standards during their training. Detail explanation of various Flight tests are clearly mentioned in Flight Training Manual published under the authority of Transport Canada.

Admission to a **General Flight Test [GFT]**

In order to be admitted to a Flight test for the issuance of a Private Pilot License – Aeroplane and meet the requirements of CAR 421.14, the candidate should present following:

1. Photo identification with signature;

2. A valid permit, license or a foreign Pilot license issued by a contracting state;

3. Proof of meeting the medical standards for the Private Pilot Licence,

4. A letter from a qualified Flight instructor certifying that:

   a. A pre-test evaluation has been completed with the candidate;

   b. The candidate is considered to have reached a sufficient level of competency to complete the Flight test for the issuance of the Private Pilot Licence, and

   c. The instructor recommends the candidate for the Flight test.

5. Evidence of having completed 35 hours total Flight time.

General – Admission to a Partial Flight Test

A partial Flight test must be conducted within 30 days following the date of the failed complete Flight test. Prior to admission to a partial Flight test, the candidate will provide the requirements of (a), (b) and (c) above, and:

1. A copy of the Flight test report for the previously failed Flight test; and

2. A letter, signed by the holder of a valid Flight Instructor Rating - Aeroplane, certifying that the candidate:

   a. Has received further training on the failed Flight test item(s);

   b. Is considered to have reached a sufficient level of competency to successfully complete the Flight test; and

   c. Is recommended by the instructor for the partial Flight test.

Letters of Recommendation

Letters of recommendation must be dated within 30 days prior to the Flight test and, in the case of a candidate recommended by a Class 4 Flight instructor, the letter must be co-signed by the supervising instructor. In the case of a re-test, the person who conducted the additional training will sign the letter of recommendation.

Aircraft and Equipment Requirements

The candidate will provide:

1. An Aeroplane for the Flight tests that:

   a. 1) has a Flight authority pursuant to CAR 507 and that authority has no operating limitations that prohibit the performance of the required maneuvers; and

   a. 2) meets the requirements of CAR 425.23 Training Aircraft Requirements - subsections (1), (2) and (3) of the Personnel Licensing Standards.

b. Appropriate current aeronautical charts and Canada Flight Supplement.

c. An effective means of excluding outside visual reference to simulate instrument Flight conditions, while maintaining a safe level of visibility for the examiner.

Flight Test

All of the Flight test items required by the Flight test report and described in this guide must be completed and the minimum pass mark for the Private Pilot Licence of 62 (50%) must be achieved. All Flight tests will be conducted when weather conditions do not present a hazard to the operation of the aeroplane, the aeroplane is airworthy and the candidate and Aircraft's documents, as required by the Canadian Aviation Regulations, are valid. It is the sole responsibility of the examiner to make the final decision as to whether or not any portion or the entire Flight test may be conducted.

Flight Instructor Rating In Canada,

In Canada, the holder of a Commercial Pilot Licence or Airline Transport Pilot Licence may have their licence endorsed with a flight instructor rating - aeroplane. Initially,

the Pilot is endorsed as a Class 4 flight instructor. This allows the Pilot to deliver flight training towards the issuance of a Recreational Pilot Permit, Private Pilot Licence, Commercial Pilot Licence, Night Rating, and VFR Over-the-top Rating. The Class 4 flight instructor may only conduct training while under the supervision of a Class 2 or Class 1 flight instructor.

After satisfying certain requirements (satisfactory flight test records, experience requirements, written exams, and flight tests), an instructor can upgrade their rating to a Class 3, Class 2, and Class 1 instructor rating. The Class 3 flight instructor does not require the supervision of a Class 2 or Class 1 flight instructor. The Class 2 flight instructor may supervise Class 4 flight instructors and act as the Chief Flight Instructor (CFI) of a flight training unit. The Class 1 flight instructor may give ground school and flight training towards the endorsement of a flight instructor rating.

In order to give instruction towards the instrument rating, multi rating, type ratings, and class conversions (for example, land plane to sea plane), an instructor rating is not necessarily required. The requirements may be limited to holding a commercial or airline transport license and having met certain experience levels (such as time on type and in class). In the case of an instrument rating, the holder of a flight instructor rating can teach it even if they do not have the experience level required for non-flight instructors. Details are contained in the Canadian Aviation Regulations, Parts 401 and 421.

Civil Aviation Safety Authority Australia CASA –

Civil Aviation Safety Authority (CASA) was established on 6 July 1995 as an independent statutory authority. Its primary function is to conduct the safety regulation of civil air operations in Australia and the operation of Australian Aircraft overseas. It is also required to provide comprehensive safety education and training programmes, cooperate with the Australian Transport Safety Bureau, and administer certain features of Part IVA of the *Civil Aviation (Carriers' Liability) Act 1959*.

The Civil Aviation Regulations 1988 and the Civil Aviation Safety Regulations 1998, made under authority of the Civil Aviation Act, provide for general regulatory controls for the safety of air navigation. The Civil Aviation Act and CAR 1988 empower CASA to issue Civil Aviation Orders on detailed matters of regulation. The CASRs 1998 empower CASA to issue Manuals of Standards which support CASR by providing detailed technical material.

Student Pilot Licence

Applicants must

- be at least 16 years of age

- Meet the general English language proficiency standard for the student Pilot licence (see CAO 40.0, paragraph 8)

- If over 18, hold a current aviation security status check.

The student Pilot licence is a permit to learn to fly. Student Pilots can fly 'solo' but are restricted to their local training area; Flights must also be authorised by their instructor.

After they have completed further training and examination including a general flying progress test, student Pilots may act as Pilot in command of an Aircraft carrying passengers, but not for hire or reward. The area restriction still applies as does requirement for Flights to be authorised by a qualified flying instructor.

Private Pilot (Aeroplane) Licence

Applicants must:

- be at least 17 years of age; and

- hold a valid English language proficiency assessment of at least level 4; and

- hold or be eligible to hold a Flight radiotelephone operator licence; and

- if over 18, have a current aviation security status check; and

- have passed a written examination and Flight test; and

- have a total of 40 hours Flight time including at least

  ▷ 5 hours of general Flight time as Pilot in Command

  ▷ 5 hours of cross country Flight time as Pilot in Command

  ▷ 2 hours of instrument Flight time

Private Pilots may fly themselves or passengers anywhere in Australia for recreational purposes and do not have to obtain prior authorisation from their instructor. Private Pilots may share operating expenses of the Aircraft with their passengers.

Commercial Pilot (Aeroplane) Licence

Applicants must:

- be at least 18 years of age; and

- hold a valid English language proficiency assessment of at least level 4; and

- hold or be eligible to hold a Flight radiotelephone operator licence; and

- have a current aviation security status check; and

- hold or be eligible to hold a Flight radiotelephone operator licence; and

- have passed a written examination (current exam consists of 7 parts) and Flight test for CPL; and

- have completed training and gained the necessary flying experience - one of the following:

  ▷ have passed an CASA approved integrated CPL course where the theory and flying training are co-ordinated and acquired 150 hours in aeroplanes with at least 70 hours as Pilot in command, 20 hours cross country as Pilot in command and 10 hours instrument Flight; or have acquired at least 200 hours Flight time including at least 100 hours as Pilot in command, 100 hours of Flight time in aeroplanes, 20 hours cross country Flight time as Pilot in command of an aeroplane and 10 hours of instrument Flight time in aeroplane.

Commercial Pilots may fly for hire or reward. Commercial Pilots are authorized to fly:

- Single Pilot Aircraft as Pilot in command while the Aircraft if engaged in any operation

- multi Pilot Aircraft as Pilot in command but for private or aerial work operations only

- Co-Pilot of an Aircraft engaged in any operation

Air Transport Pilot (Aeroplane) Licence

Applicants must:

- be at least 21 years of age; and

- hold a valid English language proficiency assessment of at least level 4; and

- have a current aviation security status check; and

- hold or be eligible to hold a Flight radiotelephone operator licence; and

- have passed a written examination (current exam consists of 7 parts); and

- hold or have held a command multi engine aeroplane instrument rating; and

- have a total of 1500 hours Flight time including at least 750 hours as Pilot of registered or   recognised aeroplanes.

- The 750 hours of aeroplane experience must include at least 250 hours of Flight time as Pilot in command; at least 500 hours of Flight time as Pilot acting in command under supervision (ICUS); at least 250 hours Flight time, consisting of at least 70 hours as Pilot in command and the balance as ICUS; and 200 hours cross country; and 75 hours instrument Flight time; and 100 hours at night as Pilot in command or as co-Pilot.

The balance of the 1500 hours of Flight time must consist of any 1 of the following:

- not more than 750 hours Flight time as Pilot of a registered aeroplane, or a recognised aeroplane

- not more than 750 hours of recognised Flight time as a Pilot of:

  ▷ a powered Aircraft, or

  ▷ a glider (other than a hang glider)

- not more than 200 hours Flight time as a Flight engineer or Flight navigator (in accordance with 5.173(7) of CAR 1988 and the balance of Flight time as described in the immediate two points above.

Air Transport Pilots may fly an aeroplane as Pilot in command or co-Pilot in any operation. An ATPL is required to command a large airline type Aircraft. Note: The above requirements apply to aeroplane Pilot licences. Similar requirements apply to helicopter Pilot licences, commercial balloon licences, gyroplane and airship licences.

The Flight Instructor Training Course

6.1 Schedule 4 of the flying school AOC requires the school to develop a course acceptable to CASA consisting of:

- A program of instruction indicating the sequence of ground and flight training periods; each period shall be identified so as to permit reference to the appropriate syllabus; and
- A detailed syllabus based on the outline specified by CASA, indicating the instructional objectives for each period of instruction or practice.

For the purposes of this CAAP, this course is identified by the term - Flight Instructor Training Course (FITC).

6.2 When a CFI is designing a FITC to satisfy the requirements of CAO 40.1.7 and

Schedule 4 of the flying school AOC, the completed FITC should; list the units and elements in the course, identify who will teach these units and elements, how they will be taught and how they will be assessed.

6.3 This CAAP provides guidance/assistance for CFI's who are undertaking this task by:

- listing applicable reference material;
- defining specific roles - Supervisor, Trainer, Trainee;
- specifying the knowledge and skills to be covered;
- specifying standards to enable competency assessments;
- providing a system for recording, assessing and managing trainee progress;
- providing a schedule of events;
- specifying each training unit and element;
- providing guidance and templates to assist in the development of detailed flying school
- specific practices and procedures; and
- specifying course entry criteria and assessment processes.

In New Zealand

Pilots Licence of New Zealand by Civil Aviation Authority of New Zealand are

Private Pilot Licence (PPL) and Commercial Pilot Licence

(CPL) and ATPL - Examination Pass Credits

Private Pilots Licence - PPL

Flight time requirements

- 50 hours total flight time
- 15 hours dual flight instruction
- 15 hours solo flight time
- 5 hours instrument time
- 5 hours dual cross country navigation
- 5 hours solo cross country navigation

Other requirements

- 17 years of age for PPL
- 16 years of age to be able to fly solo
- Class 2 medical certificate
- Passes in: Flight Radio Telephone
- PPL Aviation Law and Publications
- PPL Human Factors
- PPL Meteorology
- PPL Navigation
- PPL Principles of Flight & Aircraft Technical Knowledge

Commercial Pilots Licence - CPL

- 200 hours total flight time
- 100 hours pilot in command time
- 30 hours cross country navigation

- 15 hours dual cross country navigation

- 15 hours solo cross country navigation

- 10 hours instrument time

Other requirements

- 18 years of age

- Class 1 medical

- Passes in: CPL Aviation Law and Publications

- CPL Human Factors

- CPL Meteorology

- CPL Navigation

- CPL Principles of Flight

- CPL Aircraft Technical Knowledge

Conversion to New Zealand PPL from overseas ICAO Licence

The applicant must hold a current ICAO licence and medical and meet the minimum flight experience requirements for the issue of a New Zealand PPL. See section on

PPL requirements.

The applicant must produce their logbook, licence and medical certificate at the time of applying for their New Zealand licence.

The applicant must under go a BFR (Biennial Flight Review) with a "B" category instructor. The instructor must view the candidates logbook to assess that thecandidate has the required flight experience for a New Zealand PPL.

The instructor must also provide the candidate with a thorough briefing on New Zealand procedures and the New Zealand AIP (aeronautical information publications). The logbook assessment, evidence of the BFR, a photocopy of the candidates medical/licence is sent to the CAA (Civil Aviation Authority) along with the issue fee of $55. The CAA will send the licence directly to the candidate.

It will take about 5 working days for the licence to arrive

Flying Instructor

Flying instructors teach people how to fly aeroplanes, helicopters or other aircraft.

Tasks & duties

Flying-Instructor.jpg

Flying instructors may do some or all of the following:

- teach the principles of flight, navigation and weather
- teach the skills needed to handle aircraft
- teach students how to fly visually, at night and by using navigational instruments
- teach and follow aviation rules
- conduct pre-flight checks on aircraft with students
- prepare training programmes
- test the skills and knowledge of students
- perform cleaning or administrative duties to help run the school
- teach qualified pilots about new types of equipment
- teach qualified pilots how to operate different kinds of aircraft

Skills & knowledge

Flying instructors need to have:

- excellent flying skills
- knowledge of the technical and theoretical aspects of flying, including principles of flight (how aircraft fly) and aircraft technology

teaching skills

- decision-making skills

- communication and people skills

- knowledge of civil aviation rules and laws

- skill in flight planning and navigation

- an understanding of how weather can affect flights

Entry requirements

The first step to becoming a flying instructor is to get your Commercial Pilot Licence (CPL).

After receiving your CPL, you need to study for an aeroplane or helicopter instructor rating. To receive an entry level C-category flying instructor rating, you must have:

200 hours of flight time, with 150 hours as pilot in command at least 24 hours of flight theory study through an approved flight training programme at least 25 hours of dual flight instructor training through an approved flight training programme a pass score on flight instructor rating exams.

In USA

Pilots Licence of USA

Authority

Federal Aviation Authority **FAA**

General structure of certification

1. Private Pilot

2. Instrument rating

3. Commercial Pilot

4. Airline Transport Pilot

5. Multi-crew Pilot license

6. Other licenses, ratings, and endorsements

1. Private Pilot

The majority of Pilots hold a private Pilot license. To obtain a private Pilot license, one must be at least 17 years old and have a minimum of 35–45 hours of flight time, including at least 20 hours of instruction and 10 hours of solo flight. Pilots trained according to accelerated curricula outlined in Part 141 of the Federal Aviation Regulations may be certified with a minimum of 35 hours of flight time.[2] Private Pilots may not fly for compensation or hire. However, they may carry passengers as long as they have the appropriate training, ratings, and endorsements. Private Pilots must have a current Class III medical exam, which must be renewed every 24 or 60 months (depending on age). In addition, private Pilots must re-validate their Pilot certificates every 24 months by undertaking a flight review with a certificated flight instructor (CFI).

2. Instrument Rating

An instrument rating is technically not a Pilot certificate, but an add-on that allows a Pilot to fly in weather with reduced visibilities such as rain, low clouds, or heavy haze. When flying in these conditions, Pilots follow instrument flight rules (IFR). The training provides the skills needed to complete flights without visual reference to the ground, except for the takeoff and landing phases. In the US, all Pilots who fly above 18,000 feet above mean sea level (MSL) (a lower limit of Class A airspace) must have an instrument rating.

This rating requires highly specialized training by a certificated flight instructor (CFI) with a special instrument instruction rating (CFII), and completion of an additional written exam, oral exam, and flight test. Pilots applying for an instrument rating must hold a current private Pilot certificate and medical, have logged at least 50 hours of cross-country flight time as Pilot-in-command, and have at least 40 hours of actual or simulated instrument time including at least 15 hours of instrument flight training and instrument training on cross-country flight procedures.

3. Commercial Pilot

Commercial Pilots can be paid to fly an aircraft. To obtain a commercial Pilot license, one must be at least 18 years old and have a minimum of 250 hours of total flight time (190 hours under the accelerated curriculum defined in Part 141 of the Federal Aviation Regulations). This includes 100 hours in powered aircraft, 50 hours in airplanes, and 100 hours as Pilot-in-command (of which 50 hours must be cross-country flight time). In addition, commercial Pilots must hold an instrument rating, or otherwise they would be restricted to flying for hire only in daylight, under visual flight rules (VFR), and within 50 miles of the originating airport.

4. Airline Transport Pilot [ATPL]

Airline Transport Pilots (ATPs) must be at least 23 years old and have a minimum of 1,500 hours of flight time, including 500 hours of cross-country flight time, 100 hours of night flying, and 75 hours in actual or simulated instrument flight conditions. ATPs must also have a commercial certificate and an instrument rating. ATPs may instruct other Pilots in air transportation service in aircraft in which the ATP is rated. ATPs must have a current Class I medical exam (which is more stringent than Class II or Class III), which must be renewed every six months or one year (depending on age). Like all Pilots, they must re-validate their certificates every 24 months with a flight review.

5. Multi-Crew Pilot license

MPL Pilots must be at least 18 years old, have a minimum of 250 hours of flying training, and 750 hours of theoretical knowledge instruction. Developed by the International Civil Aviation Organization, requirements for the multi-crew Pilot license (aeroplane) (MPL(A)) were included in the 10th edition of Annex 1 to the Convention on International Civil Aviation (Personnel Licensing), which superseded all previous editions of the Annex on 23 November 2006 MPL is a significant development in training professional Pilots. It represents the first time in 30 years that ICAO had significantly reviewed the standards for the training of flight crew. The Center Air Pilot Academy in Denmark was the first FTO worldwide to graduate MPL Pilots for Sterling.

In Philippines

Pilots Licence of Philippines

Authority

Civil Aviation Authority of Philippines (CAAP) is the governmental regulatory body for civil aviation in PHILIPPINES, The CAAP is responsible for issuing all aviation licenses and certificates in Philippines.

1. Private Pilot License (PPL)/Private Helicopter Pilot License (PHPL) -

Duly notarized application

Medical release

Two I.D. pictures 1.5" x 1.5"

Certificate of Flying Time

Duly attested logbook

Theoretical examination

Checkride

License Fee

Original License Form

Radio license

Pre-Solo exam result

2. Airline Transport Pilot License (ATPL)/Commercial Pilot License (CPL)/

Commercial Helicopter Pilot License (CHPL)/Private Pilot License (PPL)/

Private Helicopter Pilot License (PHPL) - Renewal

Duly notarized application

Medical release Certificate of Flying Time

Duly attested Logbook

Checkride

License Fee

Radio license

Recurrency 121 & 135

3. Student Pilot License (SPL) –

Duly notarized application

Medical release

Two ID pictures 1.5" x 1.5"

4. Airline Transport Pilot License (ATPL) - Original

Duly notarized application

Medical release

Two I.D. pictures 1.5" x 1.5"

Certificate of Flying Time

Duly attested logbook

Theoretical examination

Checkride

License Fee

Original License Form

Radio license

5. Commercial Pilot License (CPL)/Commercial Helicopter Pilot License (CHPL)

Basic Requirements:

Applicant must be 18 years old by the time of applying for CPL.

Applicant must be fit to qualify Aviation Class II & Class I medical.

Applicant must qualify ICAO English Language Proficiency (Level 4 or higher).

Flying Requirements:

Minimum150 Hours of Flight time.

Applicant shall have cleared the necessary theory exam.

Duly notarized application

Medical release

Two I.D. pictures 1.5" x 1.5"

Certificate of Flying Time

Duly attested logbook

Theoretical examination

Checkride

License Fee

Original License Form

Radio license

Ground Schooling

CHAPTER 4
Pilots and Personal Computer

How having a Personal Computer or Laptop impacted the Aviation Industry.

Eventually integration of computers between the computers that control the Aircraft with computers on the ground will eliminate the need for Certain Aircraft controllers; and at some point eliminate the need for Pilots.

Although I'm not aware of any in existence, we are sure that a computer could calculate the best glide ratio faster than a person could in the event of a double engine failure. Not to mention GPS would find the nearest suitable Airport quicker than a Pilot with a map. Even finding a suitably unpopulated area to crash-land in such as a river could be determined with GPS maps.

So it's no longer a question of whether an Airplane could be flown entirely by computers; it's a question of reliability and acceptance. Airbus has been using fly-by-wire since 1989 without any significant problem. But not even Mr. Bill Gates himself would fly on an Aircraft flown entirely by Windows 8.

YA! It is going to cut me short here (for everyone's benefit of course). I'll conclude by saying the future of Aviation will be quite exciting. I hope others share in this excitement!

As per all Airlines Pilots must have access to a PC and needs them to check mails once in every 24Hrs. This duration may change Airlines to Airlines.

CHAPTER 5

Medical Certificates

In the United States, there are three classes of medical certifications for Pilots; such certificates are required to legally exercise the privileges of a Pilot license or certificate. Each certificate must be issued by a doctor approved by the Federal Aviation Administration to a person of stable physical and mental health.

The Three kinds are:

Third Class Medical Certificate:

It is necessary to exercise the privileges of a private Pilot license or certificate. You can also exercise the privileges of a recreational Pilot certificate, student Pilot certificate, or Flight instructor certificate with this medical certification. In the United States, it expires after 60 calendar months for someone under the age of forty years, or 24 calendar months for someone over forty.

Second Class Medical Certificate:

It is necessary to exercise the privileges of a commercial Pilot license or certificate. In the United States, it expires after 12 calendar months.

First Class Medical Certificate:

It is necessary to exercise the privileges of an Airline transport Pilot license or certificate. In the United States, it expires after (12 calendar months Under 40) (6 months over 40) for those operations requiring a First-Class Medical Certificate; 12 calendar months for those operations requiring only a Second-Class Medical Certificate; or 24 or 36 calendar months, as set forth in 61.23, for those operations requiring only a Third-Class Medical Certificate.

When a certificate is expired, it may still be used to exercise the privileges of the highest level that would not yet have expired. For example, a nine month old American first class certificate could be used as a second class certificate.

Flight Physicals

All Civilian Pilots must pass routine periodic medical examinations known informally as "Flight physicals" in order to retain the medical clearance or certification that qualifies them to fly. Military Pilots go to a Flight surgeon, an armed forces physician qualified to perform such medical evaluations. With the exception of glider Pilots, balloon Pilots and sport Pilots, civilian Pilots in the United States and most other nations must obtain a Flight physical from a civilian physician known as an Aviation Medical Examiner (AME). AMEs are physicians designated and trained by the FAA to screen individuals for fitness to perform Aviation duties. Pilot medical assessment by way of the Flight physical is an important public health function. Flying has the potential for serious consequences if not done properly and carefully. Just as it would be unwise to fly in an Aircraft that is not airworthy, it is unsafe to fly as, or with, a Pilot who is medically compromised.

Annual inspections are performed on all Aircraft to assure that they meet minimum safety standards. Routine medical exams accomplish the same goal for Pilots. When an Aircraft successfully completes an annual inspection, the inspector endorses in the logbooks to signify the Aircraft is airworthy. Similarly, when a Pilot successfully passes the Flight physical, the physician endorses the Airmen Medical Certificate which the Pilot then carries when performing Flight duties. This is then evidence that the Pilot has met the medical standards for Aircraft operation.

Types of Flight Physicals

Federal Aviation Regulations in the U.S. require Pilots and air traffic controllers to have periodic Flight physicals in order to perform their Aviation related duties. Authority for these laws comes from the CFR

(Code of Federal Regulations) parts 61 and 67. Federal regulations describe three classes of medical certificates: Class 3 medical certificates are for private Pilot duties only. They have the least restrictive medical requirements and the certificates are good for 5 years for applicants under age 40 and 2 years for those 40 and over. Class 2 medical certificates are for commercial, non-Airline duties as well as private Pilot duties. This certificate would be required of crop dusters, charter Pilots, corporate Pilots, and anyone else who flies commercially. The certificate is good for 1 year for commercial activities and 2 or 5 years for private Pilot use based on age.

Class 1 medical certificates are required for Airline transport Pilots who fly scheduled Airliners. These are the most complex examinations and include electrocardiograms (EKGs). EKGs are required at the first Class 1 medical after the applicant turns 35 and then the first medical after age 40 and yearly thereafter. Class 1 certificates are good for Airliner duties for 1 year for applicants under age 40 and 6 months for those 40 and over. Like the Class 2 certificate, however, these remain good for a full year for other commercial activities and 2 or 5 years for private Pilot duties. Detailed medical requirements for each class of Pilot exam are described in Code of Federal Regulations Part 67.

A newer Pilot classification in the United States does not require a formal Flight physical. A Pilot can fly a light sport Aircraft if they hold a sport Pilot certificate or a recreational Pilot certificate and have a U.S. driver' license from any state. Pilots with neither a driver's license nor an Airmen Medical Certificate can still fly, but Aviation duties are restricted to non-commercial activities in a glider or a balloon. The Pilot must self-endorse and certify that he/she has no known medical deficiencies which would render them incapable of Piloting an Aircraft. Sport Pilot medical requirements are described in detail in CFR 61.303

Denial of Medical Certification

Depending upon which Class certificate a Pilot wants or needs, it is possible that either the Aviation Medical Examiner or the FAA may deny a Pilot's medical certificate. This may be due to recent surgery, medication taken, non-Aviation-related offenses (such as drunk driving citations), or any other medical condition. Pilots may appeal denials up to and including formal appeals to the National Transportation Safety Board. The process of making an appeal includes meticulous documentation of a Pilot's medical condition; therapies involved in treatment, and may be accompanied by psychological evaluations and/or other data. While any Pilot may successfully make and receive approval via appeals, there are professional organizations that exist to aid Pilots in appealing the denial of a medical certificate.

The assessment process for initial applicants can be found on our Guidance for Applicants for Initial Medical Certificates in the UK flow chart.

Initial Applicant Enquiries

Initial applicant enquiries on fitness for Class 1 medical certification should be made to an aero medical Centre.

Initial Class 1 (Professional Pilot) Medical Examination

The Class 1 initial medical examination must be carried out at either the UK CAA aero medical Centre (AeMC) or NATS, Swanwick, Hampshire.

Who can apply?

An applicant for a Commercial or Multi-Crew Pilots License must be at least 18 years old, and applicants for an ATPL license must be at least 21 years old. A Class 1 Medical Certificate will be required while completing the Training for these categories of license.

Validity

UK CAA Medical Certificate Validity Table

What to Expect?

The medical examination may take up to 4 hours and includes:

Medical History - Application for Medical Certificate (MED 160)

These are a series of questions about medical history and any previous illness. You will be asked about them by your AME, and if there is any

major illness in your past, it is important to bring reports about it from your family doctor or treating specialist. Appendicitis or a broken arm is not regarded as major illnesses. Further details of the regulatory requirements can be found on our Medical Examination Standards page. You may find it helpful to print off the requirements and discuss them with your GP or Specialist. Guidance on the information your AME will require in medical reports, together with flow charts on the assessment process for a number of medical conditions can be found on our Documents for Download page.

Eyesight - Eye examination form (MED 162)

Eyesight requirements are listed in the Class 1 Visual Standards guidance material. If you wear glasses or contact lenses it is important to take your last optician's report along to the examination. An applicant may be assessed as fit with Hypermetropia not exceeding +5.0 dioptres, myopia not exceeding -6.0 2dioptres, astigmatism not exceeding 2.0 dioptres, and anisometropia not exceeding 2.0 dioptres, provided that optimal correction has been considered and no significant pathology is demonstrated. Monocular visual acuities should be 6/6 or better.

Physical Examination - Guidance on Performing Medical Examinations for AMEs

A general check that all is functioning correctly. It will cover lungs, heart, blood pressure, stomach, limbs and nervous system.

Hearing – ENT form (MED 163)

A pure tone audiometry test will evaluate your hearing. Applicants may not have a hearing loss of more than 35dB at any of the frequencies 500Hz, 1000Hz or 2000Hz, or more than 50dB at 3000Hz, in either ear separately.

Electrocardiogram (ECG) - this measures the electrical impulses passing through your heart. It can show disorders of the heart rhythm or of the conduction of the impulses, and sometimes it can show a lack of blood supplying the heart muscle. Changes on an ECG require further investigation. A report from a cardiologist and further tests (for example exercise ECG) may need to be done.

Lung function test (spirometry) - this tests your ability to expel air rapidly from your lungs. Abnormal lung function or respiratory problems, e.g. asthma will require reports by a specialist in respiratory disease (UK CAA Asthma guidance and Guidance for Respiratory Reports).

Hemoglobin blood test - this is a finger prick blood test which measures the oxygen carrying capacity of the blood. Low hemoglobin is called anemia and will need further investigation.

Urine test – you will be asked to provide a sample of urine, so remember to attend for examination with a full bladder. This test is for sugar (diabetes), protein or blood in the urine.

Typical processing time

A medical certificate is issued on the same day if all required standards are met. If the required standards are not met or further investigations are necessary before a decision on medical certification is possible this process will take longer.

Step 1: Medical Exam

Student Pilots

Prior to investing time and money in the pursuit of a Pilot's license, it is important that you be examined by a civil Aviation medical examiner to ensure that you are fit to act as Pilot in command of an Aircraft. This is always the first step that should be taken. In order to fly in Canada, you must apply for an Aviation Medical. Upon successfully passing the exam, Transport Canada will issue you with a medical certificate in addition to your student Pilot permit. This process can take from 2-3 weeks. Canadian schools cannot issue you a letter of acceptance (step 2) until you have obtained your medical.

Every ICAO country has medical examiners approved by the Canadian government to conduct Pilot medical examinations. A medical examination may also be conducted by an Aviation Medical Examiner designated by the CAA or a Contracting State of the International Civil Aviation Organization (ICAO). The appropriate medical form may be

supplied upon request from Health Canada. The list of examiners can be found at:

Licensed Pilots:

As a result of the increasing numbers of licensed Pilots coming to Canada each year to train for and receive additional license privileges, Transport Canada will now issue a Limited Term Pilot License and Medical Certificate (LTPL/MC) or Limited Term Pilot License (LTPL). The LTPL/MC is based on a valid foreign Pilot license and the medical document validating that license. The LTPL is based on a valid foreign Pilot license. As a result this will permit foreign Pilot license holders to fly Canadian registered Aircraft internationally for private recreational purposes (such as our building). The holder of this LTPL/MC or LTPL may act as Pilot-in-command or co-Pilot of any Aircraft for the sole purpose of his or her own Flight Training or Flight test. This document may also be endorsed with additional ratings.

The following conditions are applicable for the issue of a LTPL/MC:

The foreign license must have been issued by a Contracting State of ICAO and be valid under the law of the issuing state for the privileges appropriate to the specific purpose.

The foreign Medical Certificate must be valid in accordance with Canadian medical standards. (For example: In the case of a Pilot who is under 40 years of age, a LTPL/MC shall not be issued if more than 24 months has lapsed since the date of the last medical exam. In the case of a Pilot who is 40 years of age or older, no more than 12 months shall have lapsed since the last medical examination.)

The LTPL/MC validity period shall not exceed 90 days.

A LTPL/MC may only be issued to an applicant once in any 12 month period.

There will be a licensing fee and there is no requirement for a written examination.

The LTPL/MC may be endorsed for additional privileges if the required conditions are met. The following conditions are applicable for the issue of a LTPL:

The foreign license must have been issued by a Contracting State of ICAO and be valid under the law of the issuing state for the privileges appropriate to the specific purpose. A Canadian medical conducted by a Civil Aviation Medical Examiner (CAME) and assessed fit in the appropriate category by a Transport Canada Medical Advisor may validate an LTPL. The LTPL validity period shall not exceed 90 days. A LTPL may only be issued to an applicant once in any 12 month period. There will be a licensing fee. There is no requirement for a written examination. The LTPL may be endorsed for additional privileges if the required conditions are met.

CHAPTER 6

Pilot Training – Where to get it?

Becoming an Airline Commercial Pilot

General Pilot Training [Flight School Information]

If you are not very sure whether or not you would like to pursue an Aviation Career as an Aviator or Pilot, our advice to you is go to a nearby Flight Training School and take a 'Discovery Flight'. A Discovery Flight or Familiarization Flight is known by various different names depending upon the Flight School, but generally involves a 20 - 50 minute First Flight at a reduced rate to introduce you to the World of Flying. Here you will get to see the world around you from the best view window you've ever dreamed of. You will also get to hear the sounds of Aviation on the headset, as well as from the roaring engine immediately in front of you. If you wanted to become a Pilot before this first Flight, you'll most likely NEED to become a Pilot afterward! There is truly no life like it! No question the best offices are in the sky!

The views from your first Training Flight until your last Airliner Flight are amazing. The variety is unparalleled; the pristine modern Flight deck, the remote places an airplane can take you, the professionalism and team work of an Airline cockpit crew, the natural beauty seen daily by Alaskan bush Pilots, teaching a student from day one right up and until the successful conclusion of their Multi-Engine Instrument Rating, the beautiful designs of the modern business jets, the personal reward in Flying a critically ill patient to the safety of an advanced medical facility, Flying food and mail as a 'lifeline' to remote communities in northern Alaska aboard a Piper Cub, Flying all over the USA as a Southwest Airlines Pilot, Flying the new Boeing 777 Aircraft across the Atlantic Ocean as a Delta, United, or American Airlines Pilot, watching 5 skydivers fall out of your plane to meet up seconds later for their favorite Sky-Dive Assembly, Flying between beautiful mountain sides in Colorado, defending your country as an Air Force F-18 Pilot, are just a few of the hundreds of unique opportunities you will come across as a Pilot.

CHAPTER 7

Best Commercial Pilot Training Schools

Flight Safety International Pilot Training School USA

Flight Safety International Pilot Training School is the world's largest and most senior Aviation Training organization. With 40 learning centers and the largest fleet of Flight simulators, Flight Safety trains more than 75,000 Aviation professionals annually.

Flight Safety Simulation is the technology and manufacturing group of Flight Safety International. Flight Safety Simulation business units include the headquarters in Broken Arrow, OK, Visual Simulation Systems in St. Louis, MO, and Flight Safety Displays (formerly Glass Mountain Optics) in Austin, TX. Flight Safety Simulation provides the world's premier Training technology to civil and military Training organizations around the world.

Flight Safety International is a wholly-owned subsidiary of Berkshire Hathaway.

AIR RICHELIEU

With its home base in Saint-Hubert, Québec, AIR RICHELIEU is one of the leading Flight-Training centers in Canada. AIR RICHELIEU, throughout the past 20 years has managed to become the school of reference and the only one that offer you at the same time both Canadian and American licenses (FAA). From its new C172S (G1000) to the Cirrus SR20 and SR22 through the King Airs (G1000) without forgetting the famous ALSIM 200 MCC Flight simulator on which IFR renewals are now taken, AIR RICHELIEU operates the newest Aircraft, Flight Training devices and Flight simulators in the country. At the end of your Training, AIR RICHELIEU offers you the opportunity to become a Flight instructor and to commercially fly for its charter division and get hands-on experience with UNIVAIR AVIATION. To conclude and for your pleasure, AIR RICHELIEU proposes aerobatic Training.

ALGONQUIN COLLEGE

Algonquin College is the leading provider of applied, career oriented learning in Eastern Ontario. We offer more than 140 full-time programs to approximately 18,000 full-time and 30,000 part-time learners. Future Pilots need to balance education value with program cost and ensure that all is delivered within the timeframe that both the student and Industry demand. We are familiar with the expression that "timing is everything" and right now the timing could not be better for students exploring Training in the Aviation Industry. The President of the Canadian Owners and Pilots Association calls Ottawa the "Gem of Canada for Flight Training".

BRAMPTON FLYING CLUB

The Brampton Flight Centre (BFC) has been conducting Flight Training since 1946. We are very proud to have trained over 60 Indian citizens since 2006. Our Flight school is appealing because we are compatible with DGCA standards. BFC is conveniently located just 8 miles north of Brampton and 12 miles northwest of the Toronto Pearson International Airport (CYYZ). BFC operates with over 30 Flight Instructors and 22 Aircraft including the Piper Seneca, C152, C172 and in-house Flight Test Examiners. We treat everyone equally therefore the same rates apply to all students (international and local citizens alike), we have also hired international students and currently have several international students working for us. At BFC, students fly in a variety of airspace classifications, experiencing both controlled and uncontrolled environments, Canada's diverse weather allows our Pilots to gain experience they would not get in other countries and our practice area is located only five minutes from our Flight school. Please reference our website for more details www.bramptonFlightcentre.com. Judy Piccioni can help you with any questions or with your student visa when you are ready – emailinfo@bramfly.com.

COOKING LAKE AVIATION ACADEMY

Cooking Lake Aviation Academy has been established for over ten years and has many alumni Flying with Commercial Air Carriers worldwide. We are a well rounded Flight school located on the Eastern Edge of the Metro Edmonton Area, where the weather is favorable throughout the year for Flight Training and also offers winter Flight operations experience. The airport is located just outside controlled airspace within uncontrolled airspace allowing for easy transit times to and from our practice area as well the Edmonton Terminal Control Area. Our proven Flight Training methods utilizing a structured Training program will allow most students to focus on each phase of their Training in a systematic manner. We pride ourselves on the fact that our students have achieved the highest written exam test scores in the region according to Transport Canada Statistics. Our airport is located within minutes of two major towered airports with ILS and GPS approaches; IFR Training is conducted in modern autoPilot equipped Aircraft. We offer in-house Flight test examinations with our Designated Flight Test Examiner, English Language Proficiency Exams, Transport Canada Private Pilot Computer Exams, Ground Schools (Private, Commercial and IFR). Working with industry partners we offer transport category type ratings including Boeing and Airbus Aircraft. Cooking Lake has the most modern fleet of Aircraft in Western Canada with an average fleet age of 5 years or less. We offer the most advanced glass cockpit and Garmin GPS equipped Aircraft (Cessna 172SP and Diamond DA20C1 Eclipse, Piper PA44-180 Seminole) for Flight Training and maintain our Aircraft to Transport Canada Commercial Standards. Students will find themselves in relaxed friendly environment while studying towards their Flying career goals. Accommodations are located in the City of Sherwood Park which is a suburb of the City of Edmonton, full service shuttle service is provided to and from and offers close proximity to Restaurants (including international cuisine, Indian, Chinese, etc.) and local attractions including shopping malls, movie theatres and more. For students whom on their days off would like to travel into Edmonton from our student accommodation, public transit is accessible at a very minimum cost. Cooking Lake Aviation Academy offers the most competitive rates in the Edmonton Area for our product.

GFT AEROSPACE TECHNOLOGIESGFT

It is in a unique position to offer you more than just a Commercial License. GFT has a plan that will see you begin your Aviation career as a student Pilot and possibly transition into Airline operations as our sister company is a Tier Three Carrier for Air Canada in addition to our Charter and Medevac operations. GFT has been producing Professional Pilots since 1992 and continue to do so.GFT prepares Pilots for the real world of Aviation. GFT has a state of the art facility, large fleet of Cessna Aircraft, many qualified instructors and a proven program to help you achieve your goal, on time and on budget. GFT strategically located in Gander Newfoundland, Canada, is well positioned as a Flight Training facility. GFT students experience four seasons. This proves to be beneficial because students experience real world weather conditions and can avoid the label "sunshine Pilots".

GREENWOOD FLIGHT CENTRE

They are situated in the beautiful Annapolis Valley in the Province of Nova Scotia. It is located on the east coast of Canada in what is called the Maritime Provinces, in a rural community approximately an hour's drive west of the capital city of Halifax. It has been Training Pilots since 1958 and offer courses from the Recreational Permit to Multi-engine/Instrument Flight Rules Rating, including Integrated Programs. We operate Cessna 172's and Seneca Aircraft. Many graduate Pilots from our 2 year Professional Pilot diploma course continue Training for an instructor rating and in many cases gain subsequent employment at our institution.

GRONDAIR

Since 1978, our school has acquired an international reputation. We are accredited by Transport Canada and certified by ICAO (International Civil Aviation Organization) to offer the following levels Pilot licensing: Recreational, Private and Professional Pilot. We also offer the following rating: Instrument, VFR Over-the-top, Night, Multi-engine and Flight Instructor Rating. Jet transition and multi crew Training are also available.

Grondair's Pilot school is headquartered in Saint-Frédéric, Québec, where you can learn to fly in a professional, efficient and pleasant environment. Our private facilities are approved by Transport Canada

and enable you to learn NDB and GPS instrument approaches without costly delays that are typical of international airports. For controlled airspace and advance Instrument Training, the Quebec City international airport is 15 minutes Flight time from our installation.

Basic Training is offered using the classic Cessna 152 and Cessna 172. Once you have completed your courses you can also rent these planes to increase your Flight time. The Single engine IFR Training is offered using the Cessna 182RG, the planes we use annually to conduct forest fire patrols across Quebec. Finally, Professional Pilot Multi engine IFR Training is offered on planes commonly used by the Aviation industry in North America, the Cessna 310R, the Piper Navajo and the Beechcraft king Air 100. Each year, Grondair hires Pilots for forest fire patrols, sightseeing, Flight instruction and as part of our Flight crews for our chartered Flights in Canada and the U.S.A. Grondair is the only school that hires over 20 new graduates every year! And since we get to know you well, especially your skills and abilities as Pilots, Grondair is able to offer many of you employment as Pilots.

OTTAWA AVIATION SERVICES

Ottawa Aviation Services provides Aviation professionals and enthusiasts with Flight Training based on the values of the "golden age" of Aviation: "back to basics", "stick & rudder", practical Training, high level of customer service in a safety oriented environment. At OAS we do not train you to meet the minimum standards – We expect our students to exceed the government requirements. Our personable and patient instructors will encourage you to be the best and safest Pilot possible. You will experience Flying in adverse weather conditions and strong crosswinds. You will learn to operate within the environment of International airports as well as small grass strips. You will become a knowledgeable, confident and safe Pilot ready with all the basics and experiences to become a commercial Pilot.

PACIFIC FLYING CLUB

The Pacific Flying Club celebrates its' forty fifth anniversary in 2010 and is recognized as one of the premier professional Flight Training facilities in British Columbia. The not for profit Club is the only school at

Boundary Bay Airport to be an active member of both the Air Transport Association of Canada and the British Columbia Aviation Council.

Pacific Flying Club is accredited by the Private Career Training Institutions Agency of British Columbia. The Club is extremely proud to have been the first Flight Training centre in Vancouver to hold this distinction. PFC is also pleased to announce that they are in partnership with the British Columbia Institute of Technology and together BCIT and PFC are now offering "Airline & Flight Operations". We think this is a strong testament to our quality and reputation in the industry. The Club operates and maintains a fleet of 26 Aircraft including Cessna 152,172 and Piper Seneca's. Our commitment is to provide our members and students with an enjoyable, quality Flight Training environment.

Pacific Flying Club is also pleased utilize an Al Sim FTD with Level 5 King Air capabilities and Garmin 430 GPS technology. This FTD provides the most advanced simulation available at Boundary Bay Airport, maintaining the Club's stature as one of the premiere Flight Training organizations in Western Canada.

REGINA FLYING CLUB

Regina's only Flight school including an approved Flight simulator, Private, and Commercial, Night, Single and Multi-engine, Instrument and Instructor ratings, a fleet of 10 commercially registered Aircraft. The SIAST Aviation Diploma is available through the Regina Flying Club.

Our Private License costs less than the national average. Accelerated learning is possible because we run a complete operation with all top quality instructors and fully equipped Training Aircraft. South Saskatchewan has more hours of VFR Training weather and less Aircraft congestion. The Regina Flying Club gives you the best value for your Training dollar.

SELKIRK COLLEGE PROFESSIONAL AVIATION PROGRAM

The Selkirk College Aviation – Professional Pilot Diploma program has been preparing students for commercial Pilot positions in Canadian and International Airlines since 1968. Students graduate with an Aviation Diploma, Commercial Pilot License, and Group I Multi-IFR.

Additional Training components include: Multi Crew operations in an Alsim FTD, Flight physiology and psychology, High Altitude Indoctrination, team building, dispatching, use of SOP's and FOM, First Aid and CPR, four day winter wilderness survival experience, and dangerous goods Training.

SKY WINGS AVIATION ACADEMY LTD.

Sky Wings Aviation has a unique Training location for numerous reasons, starting with our predominantly good Flying weather 95% of the year and uncongested airspace. This amounts to more Flying days per year than any other site in Canada. The Red Deer Airport has a Flight Service Station, which is open 24 hours a day and is also equipped with an instrument approaches for the main runway's. Located almost equal distance from the International Airports at Edmonton and Calgary, Red Deer offers easy access for our students to both these busy environments while the local Flying area is ideal for basic Flight Training and for perfecting more advanced skills. Central Alberta is also a region of transition from the rolling foothills of the Rocky Mountains to the vast grassland of the Canadian Prairies, allowing for the exceptional experience of Mountain Flying, as in "Rocky Mountain Flying," which is available eighty miles to the West. The area located nearer to the airport includes rolling woodlands, cattle ranches and vast areas of agricultural land.

SOUTHERN SKIES AVIATION

Flanked by two crystal blue valley lakes and surrounded by world-class rock climbing, mountain biking and golfing sites, Penticton is ideally situated for the outdoor enthusiast.

Apart from this pristine environment, Penticton is home to two distinguished Aviation- Training companies, Canadian Helicopters and Southern Skies Aviation Ltd.

Southern Skies Aviation Ltd. distinguishes itself as the only Career Flight Training College in Western Canada with a Transport Canada approved Integrated Commercial Pilot Course with industry experience on all Transport Category Aircraft. Southern Skies Aviation Ltd. offers Flight Training for all licenses, ratings and endorsements.

TORONTO AIRWAYS LTD.

Toronto Airways, in central Canada (province of Ontario) is one of the largest schools in Canada. Along with our sister school, Canadian Flight Academy, we have been proud to welcome many Indian students for commercial Pilot Training over the past few years. We will meet you at the airport and help you find accommodation to suit your budget. If you get homesick for Indian culture and food, you can enjoy visiting "Little India" in Toronto for a meal, shopping and conversation with locals in this vibrant neighborhood.

Our 45 + Aircraft fleet includes the C-172s and C-152s you need to train on to be eligible to convert your hours when you return home to India. Your fees as an Indian student are the same as the fees charged to our domestic students.

Toronto Airways is a proud member of the Air Transport Association of Canada. We are registered with the provincial Government of Ontario as an accredited Private Career College.

VICTORIA FLYING CLUB

The Victoria Flying Club has been Training professional Pilots for 63 years and is located on beautiful Vancouver Island at the Victoria International Airport. We enjoy a very temperate climate which allows us to fly seven days a week year-round, providing our students with virtually uninterrupted Training. Pilots trained here have orbited the earth aboard the Space Shuttle, commanded the famous Canadian Air Force demonstration team, the Snowbirds, and are Flying with major Airlines all over the world.

Our students are able to experience Flying in a busy controlled airspace however our practice areas are located just outside the control zone so transit time is brief and Flying time is very productive. VFC is the largest school on Vancouver Island with 14 Aircraft, 13 Instructors and a 20,000 square foot facility complete with numerous classrooms, briefing rooms and a student lounge. We have considerable experience Training students from India (25 in the past three years) and are very familiar with the requirements of both our Indian students and the DGCA. Let our competent and caring staff look after you as you prepare for your career as a professional Pilot.

WATERLOO WELLINGTON FLIGHT CENTRE

Located one hour west of Toronto in the tri-cities of Kitchener/Waterloo/Cambridge WWFC has been Training Pilots since 1932. WWFC is a registered Private Career College with the Ontario Ministry of Training, Colleges and Universities and we are partnered with Conestoga community college and the University of Waterloo to provide postsecondary diploma/degrees along with commercial multi-IFR Pilot qualifications. We also offer professional Pilot Training as stand-alone programs and we have had recent experience Training students from India. Our new Training building was completed in 2009 and we have a fleet of over 25 Aircraft available for Training. Our airport has daily Airline service, with a control tower and multiple IFR approaches, yet the uncontrolled airspace of our practice area is just 5 minutes away!

WETASKIWIN AIR SERVICES LTD.

Over 35 years of successful business has earned Wetaskiwin Air Services an excellent reputation for both Training and Aircraft maintenance that extends beyond the province. Located less than 30 miles from the Edmonton International Airport (CYEG) in the City of Wetaskiwin, Alberta, Wetaskiwin Air Services offers accelerated Flight Training for Indian students. Features include immediate proximity and uncongested access to both controlled and uncontrolled airspace, short to no waiting time to access the runway, excellent student to instructor ratio and great Flying weather. Wetaskiwin Air Services can take you from no experience Flying Aircraft to a Canadian Commercial Pilot License in 8 months with proficiency and knowledge of all Flying conditions including the distinct Canadian seasons, and Flying in the prairies and the option of the Rocky Mountains. Additionally, you will train and have access to all facilities at the Wetaskiwin Regional Airport which resident business and others enthusiasts make a friendly and welcoming environment. The progressive Training methods, competent Flight instructors and an onsite highly skilled Aircraft maintenance division ensure student safety. Accommodations are within walking distance to the airport and transportation within town limits is included.

Asian Academy of Aeronautics

Asian Academy of Aeronautics (AAA) is the premier Flight Training Academy in Asia offering a wide range of courses. AAA is a privately owned company based in the Gan Island in the Republic of Maldives. (Formerly a well known RAF Base and at present a prominent touristic destination in Asia)

AAA offer Flight Training from the basic ab-initio to Private Pilot (PPL) and to the advanced Commercial Pilot License (CPL) standards. The Flight and ground Training is conducted in accordance with ICAO and JAA-FCL compliant standards as required by the Maldivian Civil Aviation Dept; (MCAD), an ICAO member state.

Financing Pilot Training Internationally

Scholarships for Pilot Training:

1. AOPA

AOPA has long been known as the most influential general Aviation organization. To help promote general Aviation, AOPA supplies scholarships to students earning a recreational, sport, or private Pilot license. The number and amounts of scholarships can vary from year to year, but range from $3,000-5,000. Scholarships are based on merit, goals and dedication to Flight Training.

Eligibility

Scholarship applicants must meet all criteria listed below.

1. Be a U.S. citizen or U.S. permanent resident

2. Be at least 16 years of age

3. Hold a current FAA Student Pilot Certificate at the time of application

4. Be a current and paid member* of AOPA at both the time of application and when the scholarship is awarded

5. Not have completed the FAA practical test/checkride at the time of application

   * the term "member" includes both voting membership and non-voting membership in AOPA.

Application Process

After completing the online application, you will receive a unique link for an online recommendation form that is specific to you. Send that exact link to two individuals and ask them to complete the online recommendation form by the application deadline (Friday, August 24, 2012 [11:59 p.m. EST]). Send the unique link to only two individuals. The online system will not accept more than two recommendations.

2. **EAA Young Eagles:**

The Experimental Aircraft Association Young Eagles program has been helping young people achieve their dreams of Flight for years. The Young Eagles offers a multitude of scholarships to members to put toward Flight Training or toward tuition for EAA Air Academy Sessions. Scholarship types and amounts vary, and are given to both pre- and post-high school students with a desire to learn to fly and/or begin a career in Aviation.

3. **Women in Aviation:**

Women in Aviation, International offers a large number of scholarships for both men and women in Aviation. Scholarships range from initial Flight Training to Airline transport Training. In the past, many Airlines have offered type rating scholarships as well as job offers to qualified candidates. Whether you're just beginning your Flight Training or looking to further your career, WAI is sure to have a scholarship for you.

Scholarships for Collegiate Flight Training Programs:

1. Women in Aviation

In addition to non-collegiate awards, WAI also has many scholarships for students in a university Flight Training program. These scholarships can sometimes be used to assist with tuition; other times, they can be used toward Flight fees. Men, don't worry- not all scholarships are reserved strictly for women.

2. NBAA

National Business Aviation Association is a highly-regarded organization in the business sector of the Aviation industry. The organization provides at least one scholarship for a student in an Aviation-related degree program at an NBAA-approved college or university. While there is an emphasis on business Aviation, general Aviation applicants may apply.

Current NBAA-Sponsored Scholarships for Students:

The Association currently offers the following scholarships to highly qualified students studying Aviation-related curricula at institutions of higher learning.

Alan H. Conklin Business Aviation Management Scholarship:

Target Candidate: Undergrad

Target Area within Business Aviation: Students pursuing a career in business Aviation management at NBAA and UAA institutions.

Total Scholarship Award: $5,000: Educational Costs

Candidate Requirements: Full-time undergraduate enrollment or acceptance into an Aviation management program at a NBAA and UAA member school; Rising sophomore or higher standing; Minimum GPA – 3.0

* US Citizenship or Permanent Resident status

Lawrence Ginocchio Aviation Scholarship:

Target Candidate: Undergrad

Target Area within Business Aviation: Aviation students who demonstrate honesty, integrity, and selflessness.

Total Scholarship Award: Five awards of $4,500: Educational Costs

Current Application Deadline: July 31,2013 – available Spring 2013

Notification/Award Period: Awarded each Fall

U.S. Citizenship Required?*: Yes

Candidate Requirements: Full-time undergraduate enrollment in an Aviation-related program at a NBAA and UAA member institution; Rising sophomore or higher standing; Minimum GPA – 3.0

* US Citizenship or Permanent Resident status

UAA Janice K. Barden Aviation Scholarship:

Target Candidate: Undergrad

Target Area within Business Aviation: Studies in Aviation-related curricula at NBAA and UAA institutions.

Total Scholarship Award: Five awards of $1,000: Educational Costs

Current Application Deadline: November 1, 2013, available Spring 2013

Notification/Award Period: Next scholarship awarded Spring, 2014

U.S. Citizenship Required?*: Yes

Candidate Requirements: Full-time undergraduate enrollment in an Aviation-related program at a NBAA and UAA member institution; Sophomore or higher standing; Minimum GPA – 3.0

* US Citizenship or Permanent Resident status

William M. Fanning Maintenance Scholarship:

Target Candidate: 1. Student enrolled in A&P Part 147 program; 2. Accepted but not enrolled in A&P program

Target Area within Business Aviation: Business Aviation Maintenance Technician

Total Scholarship Award: Two awards of $2,500: Educational Costs

Current Application Deadline: Awarded each Fall

Notification/Award Period: July 31, 2013, available Spring 2013

U.S. Citizenship Required?*: Yes

Candidate Requirements: Officially enrolled in an accredited A&P program or accepted for enrollment by an approved FAR Part-147 school.

* US Citizenship or Permanent Resident status NBAA and Conklin & de Decker established the Alan H. Conklin Business Aviation Management Scholarship to benefit undergraduates pursuing careers in business Aviation management at NBAA- and University Aviation Association (UAA)-affiliated

institutions. The scholarship was created to honor the memory of Al Conklin, U.S. Air Force veteran, co-founder of Conklin & de Decker and business Aviation leader for more than 60 years.

The Lawrence Ginocchio Aviation Scholarship was created in 2001 by NBAA and the family and friends of the late Lawrence Ginocchio to honor his outstanding personal contribution to the business Aviation community. The scholarship benefits undergraduate students officially enrolled at NBAA/UAA-member institutions.

NBAA named the William M. Fanning Maintenance Scholarship for a retired NBAA staff member who was active in maintenance issues during his nearly 20-year tenure at the Association. This scholarship annually benefits two recipients: a student who currently is enrolled in an accredited airframe and powerplant (A&P) program at an approved FAR Part 147 schools, and a second individual who is currently not enrolled but has been accepted for enrollment in an A&P program.

Education loans and Scholarships for Pilot Training in India:

Here's some information on Education loans and Scholarships for Pilot Training in India:

If you would like to be a Pilot in the Indian Air Force, you can do so by taking the NDA entrance exam after Class XII (Phys & Math). In this case your Training is free and you will be paid a decent stipend throughout your three years of Training at the National Defense Academy, followed by specialized Training at the Air Force Academy. After this, you will be commissioned as a Flying Officer and posted as a Pilot at an Air Force Station.

Note: Once you get into the air force, you cannot leave at your own discretion and there are legal tools to prevent IAF Pilots from leaving the force. Pilots cannot be released unless they are not required by the IAF and the IAF permits them to leave.

Scholarships

The following scholarships are available at and administered through IGRUA, in Rae Bareilly (Uttar Pradesh):

1. Indian Airlines scholarships

Two scholarships of Rs 4, 00,000, each given on merit-cum-means basis per batch.

2. Air India scholarships

Two scholarships of Rs 4, 00,000, each given on merit-cum-means basis per batch.

3. Rajiv Gandhi Foundation

For two women Pilots on merit-cum-means to the extent of Rs 3, 00,000 each per batch.

4. Scholarships for SC/ST candidates

Rs 2, 00,000 on Training fee.

Additional Rs 2, 00,000 by IGRUA to three SC/ST candidates per batch by selection on merit cum means basis.

Some state governments award scholarships to SC/ST candidates for Training at IGRUA. Eligible candidates may approach the respective State SC/ST Welfare Directorate for the same.

5. JRD Tata Memorial scholarships

For four students, of an amount not less than Rs 1, 00,000 on merit-cum-means basis. The JRD Tata Trust offers up to Rs 10 lakhs per year to trainees as decided by its Board of Directors.

Visit the IGRUA web site for more details.

~The Madras Flying Club offers a government scholarship as well.

Eligibility: Class X + 10+2; you must also have a Private Pilot License from the Madras Flying Club.

Address

Madras Flying Club Ltd

Madras Air Port, PO

Madras -- 600 027

~ A government scholarship for Pilot Training is available for SC/ST candidates who have completed SSC/10+2.

You may write to:

The Central Government

M/s Internal Aviation 4-A

Garden Rose, Four Bungalows

Andheri West

Mumbai -- 400 053

Education loans

Traditionally, Flying schools admitted students from affluent families. However, the trend is changing now. Flying schools as well as Airlines have reported an increase in the number of students from middle-class families. For instance, around 50 per cent of Pilots from SpiceJet's new batch are from middle-class families.

Education loans have enabled the dreams of aspiring Pilots from middle-class families to take wings.

~ Flying school-Airlines tie-ups

Various Flying schools have tied up with banks as the cost of Pilot Training is exorbitant and many interested candidates are from middle-income families. These Flying schools also have a tie-up with Airlines to provide them with students.

United Aviation, a Pilot Training school, has tied up with SpiceJet wherein it provides Pilots to the Airline. American School of Aviation had an official tie-up with defunct Kingfisher Airlines. Aerostar Aviation,

a Delhi-based Flying school has tied up with Flight Safety Academy of USA to help bridge India's Pilot shortage.

~ *Bank loans*

Pilot Training now features in the top three categories of education loans, along with MBA and hotel management.

Around 45 per cent of the educational loans furnished by Centurion Bank of Punjab in a month are for Pilot Training.

Many other nationalized banks grant educational loans to pursue commercial Pilot Training courses, the details of which can be obtained directly from such banks.

For example, State Bank of Bikaner and Jaipur offers a commercial Pilot loan, the details of which can be read at this link.

Corporation Bank also offers and Educational Loans for Commercial Pilot Training both within and outside India.

Other banks which offer student loans are State Bank of India, Canara Bank, Syndicate Bank and Punjab National Bank.

- Corp Vidya - Loan to pursue Education: TERMS AND CONDITIONS

1. **Eligibility of the Student**

   ▷ Student should be an Indian national.

   ▷ Student should have completed previous qualifying examination and secured at least 60% marks [55% for student belonging to SC/ST category] in the previous qualifying examination. He or She should have secured admission to a higher? He/She should education course in recognized institutions in India or Abroad through Entrance test/Merit based selection process/ through Management quota after completion of HSC [10+2 or equivalent]

   ▷ The Person already in gainful employment not eligible for loan under the scheme except for pursuing evening course covered under the scheme of approved Institute. If a gainfully employed person wants to pursue full time education either on study leave or by resigning from present employment, such proposals may be considered provided the applicant submits the proof in this regard to the sanctioning authority before disbursement of loan.

2. **Eligible Courses**

- For Studies in India:

    ▷ I. Approved courses leading to Graduate/Post Graduate Degree, Diploma and PG Diplomas conducted by recognized Colleges/Universities recognized by UGC/Govt/AICTE/AIBMS/ICMR etc.

    ▷ II. Courses like ICWA, CA/integrated CA -on virtual/video mode, CFA, etc.

    ▷ III. Courses conducted by IIMs, IITs, XLRI, NIFT, NID etc.

    ▷ IV. Regular Degree/Diploma courses like Aeronautical, Pilot Training, Shipping etc. approved by Director General of Civil Aviation/Shipping, if the course is pursued in India.

    ▷ V. In case of the Aircraft Maintenance Engineering/Pre Sea Training courses must be either a Degree course recognized by a competent University or Diploma course recognized by appropriate State Body to be eligible for loan.

    ▷ VI. Research course/Ph.D courses for study in India are not eligible for loan under the scheme.

    ▷ VII. Approved Courses offered in India by reputed Foreign Universities.

    ▷ VIII. Teachers Training/Nursing/B.Ed courses provided the Training institutions are approved either by Central Govt or by State Govt and such courses should lead to Degree or Diploma course and not to Certificate course.

    ▷ IX. Correspondence courses/Part time/Certificate/Short duration/Vocational/skill development study courses, off-campus courses and On-site/Partnership programme are not eligible for loan under the scheme.

- For Studies abroad:

  ▷ I. Graduation: For job oriented Professional/Technical courses offered by reputed Universities.

  ▷ II. Post Graduation: MCA, MBA, MS etc.

  ▷ III. Course conducted by CIMA- London, CPA in USA etc.

  ▷ IV. Degree/Diploma courses like aeronautical, Pilot Training, shipping etc provided these are recognized by competent regulatory bodies in India/Abroad for the purpose of employment in India/Abroad.

  ▷ V. Diploma courses for study abroad are not permitted. However, PG diploma courses for studies abroad are permitted.

  ▷ VI. Research course/Ph.D courses for study abroad are not eligible for loan under the scheme.

3. **Eligible Expenses**

  - I. Fee payable to College./School/Hostel/Examination/ Library/Laboratory fee.

  - II. Travel expenses/Passage money for studies abroad.

  - III. Caution Deposit, Building Fund/Refundable deposit, though supported by Institution bills/receipts, are not eligible.

  - IV.Purchase of books/equipments/instruments/uniforms[Refer –Note]

  - V.Purchase of computer at reasonable cost, if required for completion of the course[Refer –Note].

  - VI.Any other expenses required to complete the course like study tours, project work, thesis etc.[Refer-note]

NOTE: Hostel fees/expenses may be considered as an eligible item for finance under the Scheme. Payment of hostel fees should be made directly to the hostel authorities.

1. Reasonable lodging and boarding charges will be considered in case the student chooses/is required to opt for outside/private/paying guest accommodation.

2. In such cases, payment towards accommodation and food may be made directly to the student.

3. Insurance premium for life of student borrower.

4. Quantum of Loan

5. Studies in India - Maximum upto Rs. 10 lakh

6. Studies Abroad - Maximum upto Rs. 20 lakh

7. Margin:

   a. Upto Rs. 4 lakh - Nil

   b. Above Rs. 4 lakh - Studies in India 5%

8. Studies abroad 15%

9. Margin may be brought–in on year-to-year basis as and when disbursement are made on a pro-rate basis.

10. Security:

    a. Up to Rs. 4.00 Lakh: Co-obligation of Parent/s, Grand Parent/s (if parents are deceased). No other security.

    b. Above Rs. 4.00 Lakh & up to Rs. 7.50 Lakh: Co obligation of Parent/s Grand Parent/s (if parents are deceased) together with collateral in the form of suitable third party guarantee.

    c. Above Rs. 7.50 Lakh: Co-obligation of Parents/Grand Parents (if Parents are deceased) together with tangible collateral security along with the assignment of future income of the student for payment of installments. The loan to be fully secured after maintaining prescribed margin on respective securities.

11. In case of married person, co obliging can be either spouse, or the parents or parents -in-law.

12. 6.1 Security- Margin for various type of securities is as under:

    a. Immovable property: 35%

    b. Govt Securities (face value of NSC/KVP etc..): 25%

    c. LIC Policy (Surrender Value): 10%

    d. Deposits (Balance outstanding): 10%

13. Rate of Interest:

    a. Simple interest will be charged during repayment holiday period.

    b. Note: 1% interest concession is available during repayment holiday period if the interest is serviced as and when debited, but not later than 30 days of debit. In the event of intermittent default, concession will be extended for the period of regular interest servicing.

14. Processing Charges: No Processing Charges for studies in India

    a. Rs. 2000/- only for studies abroad to be refunded once the loan is availed Note: The charges are exclusive of applicable service tax

15. Prepayment Charges - NIL

16. Repayment

    a. For loans upto Rs.7.5 lakhs: 10 years - Fixed

    b. For loans above Rs.7.5 lakhs: 15 years -Fixed

    c. [fixing repayment tenor lower than prescribed above is not permitted]

17. Since prepayment penalty is not applicable under the scheme, borrower may prepay the loan at any time during the currency of the loan. The loan has to be repaid within a period of 10/15 years after completion of initial repayment holiday.

18. Other Guidelines

    a. Loan should be availed preferably from the Bank/Branch situated near to the place of domicile of the parents.

    b. Take over of loan from other banks is strictly not permitted.

c. Second loan may be considered for higher study in India or Abroad. In such case repayment period/holiday period of the existing loan may be extended.

d. Reimbursement of fees only for the first year of the course is permitted only for Studies in India.

CHAPTER 8

Aviation Crew

Other than Pilot there are various other personnel who equally contribute to successful air transportation. These includes all who are a part of operation of an Aircraft in Flight like ground staff, cabin crew etc.

Cabin Crew and Ground Staff

Cabin crews are the personnel responsible for the safety and care of the passengers travelling. Their main motive is to make passengers Flying experience comfortable by serving them meals and drinks, making necessary announcements related with safety, emergency, etc.

Various courses are available for the same. The certification courses are also provided by IATA that are highly valued.

Airport ground staff encloses almost every service provided at the airport. The ground staffs are trained to provide services like loading and unloading of passengers, crew and baggage. Handling of baggage and cargo are also categorized as freight and material movers.

CHAPTER 9

Aircrafts

(SINGLE ENGINE/MULTI ENGINE/PROP/TURBO PROP/JET)

Depending upon the seating capacity, Aircraft performance, weights, limits and the type of the Engine Aviation Aircraft fleet can be classified among following-

1. Single Engine Aircraft

2. Turbo Prop

3. Multi Engine Aircraft

4. Jet Aircrafts

Single Engine Aircraft

Many Airplane Manufactures are making private Air planes for the use of corporate Piston Engines and Trainer Aircraft are Single Engine Planes. These Airplane manufactures typically build these types of Aircraft with lightweight material and an engine that is powerful enough to withstand the weight and drag of the Airplane. Airplane manufacturers who specialize in Single Engine Airplanes include Cessna, Piper, Dimond, VisionAire, Socata and Grob. There are more than 100 manufactures world wide who typically build these types of Aircrafts.

Turboprop

Most of the Turboprops are so popular small Aircrafts as they can even Land on unpaved runways and are very economical in use. These Aircrafts are Ideal for short to medium distance Flights, greater fuel efficiency and less expensive than other Jet Aircrafts.

Turboprops provide varied range in Aircrafts having capacity from 4 Seater up to 60 Pax. Turboprops fall in 2 categories – Executive Turboprop and Commuter Turboprops. These are most preferred because of their flexibility and ability to Fly out of small Airports and having Runways not suitable for larger jets. Major manufacturers of Turboprops are Cessna, Piper, Hawker Beechcraft, Vulcanair Examples: King Air C90, King Air B200, Piaggio P-180, Dornier 228 etc.

Multi-Engine Aircraft

As Aircraft design evolved, the search for more power, longer Flight and better Aircraft performance led to Multi-Engine Aircrafts format. If one engine was good, two or more must be better. It was that enthusiasm for performance and power that ultimately allowed Simple machines such as the Wright Flier to evolve into the airliners that begin stitching the world together. Rapidly progressing Aircraft Technology walked hand-in-hand with Light weight Aircraft Engine Technology making possible Aircraft that were increasingly fast and more powerful. The Technological frontier was to find new ways to utilize the Airplane. Then the goal became more people, more Cargo, and greater distances.

Major manufacturers of Turboprops are Cessna, Piper, Hawker Beechcraft, Vulcanair Examples: Piper P 34, P 68, King Air C90, King Air B200, even Airbus 340 and Boeing 747.

Jet Aircrafts

Now a days there is a huge choice of modern Private Jets Aircrafts for personal use and rentals, Private Jets Aircrafts come in various shapes and sizes, from the new range of light Jets to the long-range heavy jets. As a Jet Pilot of the Private Jet experience and enjoy the ultimate in superb in-Flight luxury and stress free travel. On board, you will enjoy complete privacy, from discreet personnel and a level of security not offered by other Airlines. As Jet Pilot Fly when and where you want, choose from thousands of Airports worldwide, choose dedicated lounges and VIP terminals that provide discreet and secure check-in procedures.

Private Jet Aircraft Types ready to fly are Private Helicopters, Very Light Private Jets, Light Private Jets, Medium Private Jets, Super Medium Private Jets, Heavy Private Jets, Jumbo Private Jets.

CHAPTER 10

Best Paying Flying Jobs

The Airline Industry has been going through a rough transition for years now. From buttoned-down security to sky-high gas prices, it's been a bumpy ride. Still, the fact remains that people want to travel and there are plenty of Jobs available at Airlines, Airports, Airplane companies and security organizations around the globe. Where might your talents fit into the Aviation industry?

Many people wish for the glamorous lifestyle and income of a Pilot. But, do Pilots always wear crisp Uniforms and make the big Bucks? Not necessarily, according to to Aviation Industry Experts "There's a huge variation in pay depending on whether you're Flying a float plane for a regional commuter company or Flying 747s for United. Regional Airlines sometimes pay $20 per hour and only when the engine is on." that too with only 1000 hours of engine time a year, that hourly rate can come close to minimum wage.

Fortunately, you don't have to wait to fly Jumbo Jets if want to work in Aviation. In fact, if you like doing math, mechanical work or security tasks, here are some in-demand job options, that are also some of the best-paid in the industry.

1. Director of Aerospace Program Management

Median Annual Salary: $1,10,000

Aerospace is second only to petroleum engineering in pay." That's why the director of an aerospace engineering program management team can earn well into the six figures. This person likely has a Graduate Degree in Business, such as an MBA, in addition to their degree in engineering. Directors are involved in developing the company's business strategy, negotiating contracts to build Aircraft and taking responsibility for company profitability.

2. Airline Pilot, CoPilot or Flight Engineer

Median Annual Salary: $70,000

Most Pilots used to receive their Training in the military, but in recent years a college degree and Training from an FAA-certified Flight Training school has become more common among new hires. And, while many may pay less, there are plenty of jobs for Pilots besides passenger Airline gigs. According to the Bureau of Labor Statistics (BLS), about 34 percent of commercial Pilots use their time in the air to dust crops, test planes, monitor traffic, fight fires and perform other non-typical functions.

3. Aerospace Project Engineer

Median Annual Salary: $52,000

An aerospace project engineer must not only understand the ins and outs of aerospace engineering, but they must have the personal and organizational skills to lead a team through a project. A project engineer is likely involved in managing the budget for a project, hiring and Training staff, checking their team's work and other administrative tasks.

4. Aircraft Maintenance Manager

Median Annual Salary: $44,200

Once again, this is a job position that requires both technical skill and a knack for leading teams. A maintenance manager is a knowledgeable professional who ensures that their teams perform maintenance regularly and according to regulatory guidelines. The manager schedules a staff of technicians and likely does much of the hiring and Training of their team.

Find Aircraft Maintenance Jobs

5. Air Traffic Controller

Median Annual Salary:$32,500

Lee notes that air traffic controller is one of the best-paying jobs you can have with an associate's degree. It's well known for causing sky-high stress levels and requiring a tremendous amount of mental focus. But, did you know that, depending on the airport, the work is separated out between controllers for ground movement, take-off, en route Flight time, landing and more? The competition for these lucrative, steady job positions is steep, though the BLS expects a wave of retirement in the coming years that should open up more positions to younger controllers.

A standard Pilot's Job Description

Minimums:

Must meet all Pilot Flight time requirements set forth to hold Commercial Pilot Certificate with Multi-Engine Airplane & Instrument rating

- FCC Restricted Radiotelephone Operator's Permit

- Current First Class Medical certificate

- Must have a valid passport

- At least 21 years of Age

- Legally authorized to work

- Must be able to read, speak and write fluently in the English Language

- Comfortable and effective with public speaking

Description:

Job Objective:

All Pilots are responsible for safe, economical, consistent and legal operation of Company Aircraft. They are required to comply with all applicable federal regulations as well as Compass Airlines policies, standards and procedures.

Essential Job Functions:

1. All Pilots are directly responsible for the safe, legal and consistent operation of the Aircraft, in accordance with all federal regulations and Company policies, standards and procedures.

2. Pilots in command of an Aircraft are directly responsible for and are the final authority as to the safe, legal and consistent operation of that Aircraft, in accordance with all federal regulations and Company policies, standards and procedures.

3. Pilots must operate, monitor, analyze and/or timely and appropriately react to all Aircraft operational functions such as Aircraft performance, internal and external communications, air traffic and climate conditions.

4. Pilots must perform Flight operations tasks including Aircraft takeoff, climb, cruise, descent, approach, landing, taxi-in and parking in accordance with FAA mandated standards.

5. Pilots must maintain expert knowledge of assigned Aircraft equipment type and current operational procedures.

6. Pilots must economically coordinate tasks to permit a number of functions, including but not limited to, Flight fueling, loading, passenger handling, and associated duties to transport passengers and cargo in a safe manner in accordance with Company policies, standards and procedures and appropriate federal regulations.

7. Pilots must timely and professionally address, as appropriate, passengers on the Aircraft and lead all crew activities related to safety.

8. Pilots must professionally and timely coordinate with others, both in the cockpit and in other operational departments.

9. Pilots are expected to present a professional image in all public environments as a key representative of the Company to both external customers and internal employees.

10. Pilots must maintain currency requirements with regard to medical, Training, and hourly Flight requirements.

11. Pilots must perform other duties as assigned.

Working Conditions:

A Pilot's working environment is subject to varying climate conditions, air turbulence, time zone changes, altitude changes, changing locations, variable hours and working conditions, dry air, jet fuel and exhaust fumes, and noise levels from engines and other ground equipment. Pilots experience long periods of sitting with exposure to bright sunlight as well as the conditions already mentioned. The position requires physical exertion such as pulling, pushing, kneeling, twisting, climbing, squatting, pinching, grasping, bending, walking, and lifting of bags and equipment. The position involves ascent and descent of jetbridge stairs and other airport facilities. Pilots must be able to hear and comprehend both spoken voice and radio communication with a range of minimal-to-excessive background noise. Pilots require good hand/eye coordination, visual acuity, color discrimination, and depth perception to fly the Aircraft, read approach plates under varying conditions and correctly read, locate and access various switches, valves, knobs, and other Aircraft controls. Pilots must be able to perform duties in an environment with potentially lowered oxygen pressure.

Applicants must maintain a high level of alertness during regular and emergency Aircraft operations. They must have the ability to communicate clearly and effectively in English, both in writing and verbally, under all circumstances.

Applicants must read and comprehend written instructions and procedures and understand verbal instructions. They must have excellent judgment, interpersonal, organizational, and leadership skills and the ability and inclination to solve problems. Applicants must have a highly approachable demeanor and be comfortable with public speaking and addressing large groups of people. They must possess basic computer skills. They must be willing to work long hours including evenings, weekends, holidays, and extended hours away from home and be able to work on an on-call basis with little notice.

Applicants also must be able to travel freely in and out of all locations served by Compass Airlines without restriction.

This position is a Federal Aviation Administration Covered position, which is subject to mandated alcohol and drug testing. Federal regulations require applicants to submit fingerprints for a criminal history investigation. Applicants must pass a pre-employment drug test, background check, PRIA records check and medical review.

CHAPTER 11
Pilots Interview Questions Best-Paying Flying Jobs

Pilots have many simultaneous responsibilities during Flight. What can you tell me about this?

During the Flying time, the Pilots have to deal with many tasks at the same time. The Pilots are the person who navigate the Flight schedule, observe and direct the crew's activities, check and applying the instruction in Flight. Beside they also have to check weather condition and give suitable solutions with each case. In addition, they also have to monitor altitude and air traffic. These simultaneously tasks are very difficult and stressful so the Pilot is required of outstanding multi- tasking skills and high concentration ability.

How would you behave as the Pilot of a plane during an emergency?

Answer: Describe first what your emotional response would be. In the interview the chance to become a Pilot is coming near to you if you can give a clear well example with the detail preferable demonstration of Pilot tasks. Let them see that you can keep your mind be stable and poise; you can persuade all members in the crew follow your instructions even in the hard situation such as emergency procedures.

What is more important to you: the money or the work?

Answer samples

1. Money and work both are like siblings. But I believe when you work hard; money will flow to you. So work is more important than money. Only hard work can help you put another feather in your success cap.

2. I believe they are equally important to our well-being. Certainly both. Even though Work is Worship money makes livelihood. Work follows money and money follows work. So, without existence of one another we can't be achievable. However I can adjust for money up to some extent if the work is really challenging and doing which gives me job satisfaction.

What are your career goals?

1. The reasons of this question: This question will test your ability and ambition to develop yourself as well as the ability to plan for the future.

2. Levels of career goals:

   You are not sure about your goals, then answer: I'm rather busy with my duties and goals of the Company; as a result, I haven't focused much on my long-term personal goals.

   You have goals not or very little relating to the current job: For example, you are applying for a sales manager, but your career goal is to become the head of marketing department in the next 5 years.

   Current job oriented career goals: For example, you are working as a sales manager, you goal is to become the area sales manager in the next 2 years and in the next 5 years, you will be the regional sales manager.

   Note that long-term goals must be set for the next 3-5 years.

   a. When you have identified your goals, you need to answer the following questions:
      - Are those goals suitable to the job you are currently applying for?

- Are those goals helpful to your current job?

- Are those goals helpful to the development of your current job in the next 3-5 years?

b. How to achieve those goals?
- Identify what you have to do to achieve your goals?

- In the next 6 months, 1 year, 2 years, what will you do?

Tell me about yourself

Steps

Step 1: Give a brief introduction about yourself:

For example: My name is Peter. I graduated from XYZ University with bachelor degree in Sales. After 5 years working as a Sales Manager, I have well experienced in Training, mentoring and motivating other sales personnel to achieve the goals of the Company.

Step 2: Give a brief summary of your experience in your latest positions:

Give a summary of 2-3 latest companies that you have worked for and companies that have helped you succeed with your new jobs.

For example: recently, I have worked for ABC Company as Sales Manager for North-East Region. With my skills from Training courses, I developed many sales campaigns which contributed much to the development of new customers and maintenance of current customer base. After 6 months, my sales force and I did regain the company's market and promote the sales revenue up by 37%.

Step 3: Connect your ability to the employer's requirements:

Never assume that the employer will by himself be able to connect all of your abilities to the job requirements.

Step 4: Make a concerning question:

With a concerning question, it will help you gain "control" of the interview. You may reduce the stress of the interview with such questions.

Tell me about a time when you failed?

Answer tips

It is certainly that anyone fails sometime, especially at work. For example, fail to comply with the regulations, fail to meet the deadline, fail to persuade others, fail to meet the goals….What matters more is what you learn from such failure, and the interviewer is planning to investigate that.

There are various reasons to failure: objective or subjective, a fraud, a wrong action, an omission or a lack of capacity…you don't need to be too cautious about these, as if you learn from your failure, then there is nothing to worry about.

In answering this question, first, state a situation when you fail to do something (It is better if the reason is not your subjective intention). Then state how you realized that and dealt with that.

What can you do for us that other candidates can't?

Answer tips/answer samples:

After all, the benefits of you are the amount of value you may contribute to the organization. The interviewer decides you are the best candidate just because you are potential to make the most contribution to their organization. So, this question falls among those of the most importance. By asking this question, the interviewer is questioning about your skills and abilities that may help their organization, your special talent that differentiate you from other candidates.

To answer this question successfully, first you have to sum up the key requirements of the current job. Then come how your past experience is useful to the job; How the skills are related and qualified to resolve all the issues in connection with the job; how your knowledge and personality are suitable for the job. Put them in logical order, support them with your confident tone and structure them soundly to show that you are very firm about what you can do for them.

If you were hiring a person for this job, what would you look for?

Answer tips

Be careful to mention traits that are needed and that you have.

That can be: Qualification, attitude, team spirit, sincerity, and spirit.

Answer sample: I would look for good communication skill and for great dedication towards job and responsibility to work in under pressure also.

- Determine trends that are happening in your industry and how to face/solve them.

- Attributes/traits/abilities related to this job and how to get them.

- Review job specs, job description in job ads for this position and try to think how to prove your capabilities.

- Research the employer profiles thoroughly, the aims of their recruitment and what are your task/roles.

What is the importance of proficiency in several languages for a Pilot?

Answer: English language may be enough with a private Pilot who only needs to understand control towers. But other Pilots, who fly publicly, knowing more than one language is the need and useful.

Pilots have many simultaneous responsibilities during Flight. What can you tell me about this?

Answer: Pilots take responsibility to navigate the Flight, view and guide the activities of the team, check instruments, and keep track of the weather, control the height and air traffic. Performing all these and more, often at once, requests salient multi-tasking abilities and strong concentration.

How would you behave as the Pilot of a plane during an emergency?

Answer: Express your feeling first. It is best to prove through examples, that you can keep your calmness during such problems, and you can self-control the emergency situation and assign tasks for team members if necessary.

What is your greatest weakness?

For example: I am a perfectionist and therefore, I rarely believe in anyone who can work as well as me. As a result, I am afraid to delegate important tasks to others.

Why should we hire you?

One of the best ways to answer this question is to make a short list of all your advantages and create a paragraph that would point out the positive aspects that you would bring to the new job position.

One of the points that you can raise is the similarity of the job profile you are aiming for at the company to the job profile you enjoyed in your previous job.

You can also draw the interviewer's attention to your key skills and strengths, namely – quick learning, excellent communication skills, etc.

In addition, your professional ambitions should be made clear – the motivation and dedication that you have for the profession and the opening position.

What motivates you to do your best on the job?

Tips

This is a personal trait that only you can say, but good examples are: Challenge, Achievement, Recognition

For any person motivation is the main factor which should make him work in an efficient manner.

And that motivation could be done my some rewards for doing good job, some encouragements etc. Moreover an employees good work must be acknowledged by his employer, which would definitely boost him to work more harder to get more acknowledgements.

Answers

1. I was motivated both by the challenge of finishing the projects on time and by managing the teams that achieved our goals.

2. I want to be successful in my job, both for my own personal satisfaction and for my employer.

3. I've always felt that it's important, both to me personally, and for the company and the clients, to provide a positive customer experience.

What are your biggest strong points?

This question will help polishing your qualification to the requirements of the employer.

1. Steps to answer this question:

    a. Identify which you are good at:

       • Knowledge;

       • Experience;

       • Skills;

       • Abilities.

    b. Prepare a list of your strong points:

    c. Review the recruitment requirements:

    d. Make a list of your strong points in your resume/cover letter:

    e. Prepare persuasive answers to the question of the employer about strong points:

You do not only state your strong points to the employer but must also provide evidence for them by references or records attached with your application form.

Strong points that the employer may concern about:

- Great communication skills;

- Ability to adapt to the change in company culture;

- Ability to solve problems flexibility;

- Hard-working;

- Ability to learn from failure;

- Group work spirit

What experience do you have in this field? or Do you have any actual work experience?

Answer tips

- Speak about specifics that relate to the position you are applying for. If you do not have specific experience get as close as you can

- If you are being asked this question from your employer then you can explain your experience. Tell the employer what responsibilities you were performing during your job. You can tell what programs you developed and what modules you worked

CHAPTER 12
Aviation Organizations

(INTERNATIONAL AVIATION ORGANIZATIONS)

ICAO

The International Civil Aviation Organization (ICAO), is a specialized agency of the United Nations. It codifies the principles and techniques of international air navigation and fosters the planning and development of international air transport to ensure safe and orderly growth. Its headquarters are located in the Quartier International of Montreal, Quebec, Canada.

The ICAO Council adopts standards and recommended practices concerning air navigation, its infrastructure, Flight inspection, prevention of unlawful interference, and facilitation of border-crossing procedures for international civil Aviation. In addition, the ICAO defines the protocols for air accident investigation followed by transport safety authorities in countries signatory to the Convention on International Civil Aviation, commonly known as the Chicago Convention.

As of November 2011, there were 191 ICAO members, consisting of 190 of the 193 UN members.

The ICAO defines an International Standard Atmosphere (also known as ICAO Standard Atmosphere), a model of the standard variation of pressure, temperature, density, and viscosity with altitude in the Earth's atmosphere.It also standardizes certain functions for use in the Airline industry, such as the Aeronautical Message Handling System (AMHS), making it a standards organization.

FAA

The Federal Aviation Administration (FAA) is the national Aviation authority of the United States of America. An agency of the United States Department of Transportation, it has authority to regulate and oversee all aspects of civil Aviation in the U.S. The Federal Aviation Act of 1958 created the organization under the name "Federal Aviation Agency", and adopted its current name in 1966 when it became a part of the United States Department of Transportation.

The FAA's roles include:

Regulating U.S. commercial space transportation.

Regulating air navigation facilities' geometry and Flight inspection standards.

Encouraging and developing civil aeronautics, including new Aviation technology.

Issuing, suspending, or revoking Pilot certificates.

Regulating civil Aviation to promote safety, especially through local offices called Flight Standards District Offices.

Developing and operating a system of air traffic control and navigation for both civil and military Aircraft.

Researching and developing the National Airspace System and civil aeronautics.

Developing and carrying out programs to control Aircraft noise and other environmental effects of civil Aviation.

The FAA is divided into four "lines of business" (LOB).Each LOB has a specific role within the FAA.

Airports (ARP):-Plans and develops projects involving airports, overseeing their construction and operations. Ensures compliance with federal regulations.

Air Traffic Organization (ATO):-Primary duty is to safely and efficiently move air traffic within the National Airspace System. ATO employees manage air traffic facilities including Airport Traffic Control

Towers (ATCT) and Terminal Radar Approach Control Facilities (TRACONs).

Aviation Safety (AVS):-Responsible for aeronautical certification of personnel and Aircraft, including Pilots, Airlines, and mechanics.

Commercial Space Transportation (AST):-Ensures protection of U.S. assets during the launch or reentry of commercial space vehicles.

JAA

The Joint Aviation Authorities(JAA), was an associated body of the ECAC representing the civil Aviation regulatory authorities of a number of European States who had agreed to co-operate in developing and implementing common safety regulatory standards and procedures. It was not a regulatory body, regulation being achieved through the member authorities.

In implementing the so-called FUJA Report, the JAA had entered into a new phase as of 1 January 2007. In this new phase the former "JAA" had become "JAA T" (Transition). JAA T consisted of a Liaison Office (JAA LO) and a Training Office (JAA TO). The offices of JAA LO were located in the premises of European Aviation Safety Agency (EASA) in Cologne, Germany.

The JAA started as the Joint Airworthiness Authorities in 1970. Originally, its objectives were only to produce common certification codes for large aeroplanes and for engines in order to meet the needs of European industry and international consortia (e.g., Airbus). After 1987 its work was extended to operations, maintenance, licensing and certification/design standards for all classes of Aircraft.

EASA

The European Aviation Safety Agency (EASA) is a European Union (EU) agency with regulatory and executive tasks in the field of civilian Aviation safety. Based in Cologne, Germany, the EASA was created on 15 July 2002,and it reached full functionality in 2008, taking over functions of the Joint Aviation Authorities (JAA). European Free Trade Association (EFTA) countries have been granted participation in the agency.

The responsibilities of EASA include to conduct analysis and research of safety, authorising foreign operators, giving advice for the drafting of EU legislation, implementing and monitoring safety rules (including inspections in the member states), giving type-certification of Aircraft and components as well as the approval of organisations involved in the design, manufacture and maintenance of aeronautical products.

The member states are Austria, Belgium, Bulgaria, Cyprus, Czech Republic, Denmark, Estonia, Finland, France, Germany, Greece, Hungary, Iceland, Ireland, Italy, Latvia, Liechtenstein, Lithuania, Luxembourg, Malta, Norway, Poland, Portugal, Romania, Slovak Republic, Slovenia, Spain, Sweden, Switzerland, The Netherlands and The United Kingdom.

ECAC

The European Civil Aviation Conference (ECAC) or Conférence Européenne de l'Aviation Civile (CEAC) is an intergovernmental organization which was established by the International Civil Aviation Organization (ICAO) and the Council of Europe. It is located in Neuilly-sur-Seine/Paris in France. Founded in 1955 with 19 Member States at the time, ECAC counts today 44 members, including all 27 EU, 30 of the 31 European Aviation Safety Agency and all 39 EUROCONTROL Member States.

ECACp romotes the continued development of a safe, efficient and sustainable European air transport system..

Its strategic priorities are safety, security and the environment.

ECAC Member States are: Albania, Armenia, Austria, Azerbaijan, Belgium, Bosnia and Herzegovina, Bulgaria, Croatia, Cyprus, Czech Republic, Denmark, Estonia, Finland, France, Georgia, Germany, Greece, Hungary, Iceland, Ireland, Italy, Latvia, Lithuania, Luxembourg, Malta, Moldova, Monaco, Montenegro, Netherlands, Norway, Poland, Portugal, Romania, San Marino, Serbia, Slovakia, Slovenia, Spain, Sweden, Switzerland, the Republic of Macedonia, Turkey, Ukraine and United Kingdom.

CAA

The CAA has been envisaged as an autonomous regulatory body which will replace the DGCA and will meet standards set by the UN's International Civil Aviation Organisation (ICAO). The CAA will have separate departments to deal with safety, economic regulation and grievance resolution, as well as a full-fledged environment department. It will also have an independent accident investigation bureau. The Authority will also have the autonomy to recruit staff.

Currently, the DGCA is understaffed and does not have any recruitment powers. The CAA will have administrative and financial powers similar to those of the American FAA. These powers will redefine the regulator's role and better equip it to face the challenges of the growing Aviation sector in the country. Employees working with DGCA will be transferred to the CAA.

The CAA would be self-financing and have a separate fund called the 'Civil Aviation Authority of India Fund' that would finance its entire expenses. It would have a Chairperson, a Director General and 7-9 members appointed by the Central Government. These members will be qualified in the fields of Aviation safety, Aircraft engineering, Flight standard operations, aerodromes, air navigation systems and air space management.

ATAC

ATAC is committed to providing its clients world-class modeling, simulation, and analysis for Aviation. With over 30 years of experience in modeling some of the most complex airports, airspace, and Aircraft noise challenges, and a product portfolio recognized worldwide for its ability to accurately simulate current and future Aviation systems, we invite you to discover how ATAC can help answer your most complex Aviation questions.

ATAC has solutions and products available for immediate application for:

Airports

Air Traffic Service Providers

Military Aviation Operations Organizations

Aviation Operations Research Professionals

ATAC's role as the lead software developer and system integrator of the FAA's Integrated Noise Model (INM) supplies in-depth insight into the model's capabilities, limitations, and use. ATAC also has a major role in the development of the Aviation Environmental Design Tool (AEDT), the FAA's next generation environmental modeling software, spanning local and global noise and emissions analyses. ATAC's FAA-funded research are aimed at improving the capabilities of the INM and the AEDT.

IATA

The International Air Transport Association (IATA) is an international industry trade group of Airlines headquartered in Montreal, Quebec, Canada, where the International Civil Aviation Organization is also headquartered. The executive offices are at the Geneva Airport in Switzerland.

IATA's mission is to represent, lead, and serve the Airline industry. IATA represents some 240 Airlines comprising 84% of scheduled international air traffic. The Director General and Chief Executive Officer is Tony Tyler. Currently, IATA is present in over 150 countries covered through 101 offices around the globe.

IATA was formed on 19 April 1945, in Havana, Cuba. It is the successor to the International Air Traffic Association, founded in The Hague in 1919, the year of the world's first international scheduled services.

IATA's stated mission is to represent, lead and serve the Airline industry. All the Airline rules and regulations are defined by IATA. The main aim of IATA is to provide safe and secure transportation to its passengers.

DGCA

The Directorate General of Civil Aviation (DGCA) is the Indian governmental regulatory body for civil Aviation under the Ministry of Civil Aviation. This directorate investigates Aviation accidents and incidents. It is headquartered along Sri Aurobindo Marg, opposite Safdarjung Airport, in New Delhi. The Government of India is planning to replace the Organisation with a Civil Aviation Authority (CAA), modelled on the lines of the American Federal Aviation Administration DGCA has fourteen Regional Airworthiness Offices (RAO) at Delhi, Mumbai, Chennai, Kolkata, Bangalore, Hyderabad, Cochin, Bhopal, Lucknow, Patna, Bhubaneshwar, Kanpur, Guwahati and Patiala. It has also five Regional Air Safety offices located at Delhi, Mumbai, Chennai, Kolkata and Hyderabad. It has a Regional Research and Development Office located at Bangalore and a Gliding Centre at Pune.

List of Abbreviations

ATPL	Airline Transport Pilot License
DGCA	Directorate General of Civil Aviation
CAA	Civil Aviation Authority
CAR	Civil Aviation Regulations
CARs	Canadian Aviation Regulations
ATC	Air Traffic Control
DGR	Dangerous Goods Regulation
EASA	European Aviation Safety Agency
EW	Empty Weight
FAA	Federal Aviation Administration
GA	general Aviation
ICAO	International Civil Aviation Organization
IATA	International Air Transport Association
NOTAM	notice to airmen
CASA	Civil Aviation Safety Authority
TCCA	Transport Canada Civil Aviation
SPL	Student Pilot License
PPL	Private Pilot License
CPL	Commercial Pilot License
A&E	Architecture and Engineering
A/C	Aircraft
A/G	Air to Ground
A/H	Altitude/Height
AAA	Airport Airspace Analysis
AAC	Mike Monroney Aeronautical Center
AADC	Airport Average Daily Capacity
AAF	Airway Facilities Service

AAF	Army Air Field
AAF-1	Director of Airway Facilities
AAI	Arrival Aircraft Interval
AAI	FAA Office of Accident Investigation
AAL	Alaska Region
AAM	Office of Aerospace Medicine
AAMS	Aircraft Arrival Management System
AAP	Advanced Automation Program
AAR	After Action Review
AAR	Airport Acceptance Rate
AAR	Airport and Aircraft Safety Research and Development
AAS	Advanced Automation System
AASR	Aging Aircraft Safety Rule
AAT	Associate Administrator for Air Traffic
ABA	FAA Office of Financial Services
ABA	Office of Budget
ABDIS	Automated Data Interchange System Service
AC	Advisory Circular
ACAA	Air Carrier Association of America
ACAIS	Air Carrier Activity Information System
ACAS	Aircraft Collision Avoidance System
ACC	Airports Consultants Council
ACC	Area Control Center
ACCT	Accounting Records
ACD	Automatic Call Distributor
ACDO	Air Carrier District Office
ACE	Central Region
ACEP	Airport Capacity Enhancement Plan
ACF	Area Control Facility
ACFO	Aircraft Certification Field Office
ACFT	Aircraft
ACI-NA	Airports Council International-North America
ACID	Aircraft Identification
ACIP	Airport Capital Improvement Plan
ACIP	Automated Conformity Inspection Process
ACLS	Automatic Carrier Landing System

ACLT	Actual Landing Time Calculated
ACO	Aircraft Certification Office
ACO	Associate Contracting Officer
ACO	Office of Airports Compliance and Field Operations
ACR	FAA Office of Civil Rights
ACRP	Airport Cooperative Research Program
ACSEP	Aircraft Certification Systems Evaluation Program
ACT	William J. Hughes Technical Center
AD	Airworthiness Directive
ADA	Air Defense Area
ADAP	Airport Development Aid Program
ADAS	Automated Weather Observing System Data Acquisition System
ADAS	AWOS Data Acquisition System
ADC	Air Defense Command
ADCCP	Advanced Data Communications Control Procedure
ADDA	Administrative Data
ADDS	Aviation Digital Data Service
ADF	Automatic Direction Finding
ADI	Automatic De-Ice and Inhibitor
ADIC	ATS Interfacility Data Communications
ADIN	AUTODIN Service
ADIZ	Air Defense Identification Zone
ADL	Aeronautical Data Link
ADLO	Air Defense Liaison Office
ADLY	Arrival Delay
ADM	Aeronautical Decision Making
ADO	Airline Dispatch Office
ADO	Airport District Office
ADP	Automated Data Processing
ADS	Automated Distribution System
ADS	Automatic Dependent Surveillance
ADS-B	Automatic Dependent Surveillance-Broadcast
ADSIM	Airfield Delay Simulation Model
ADSY	Administrative Equipment Systems
ADTN	Administrative Data Transmission Network
ADTN2000	Administrative Data Transmission Network 2000

ADVO	Administrative Voice
AEA	Eastern Region
AED	Automated External Defibrillator
AEDT	Aviation Environmental Design Tool
AEE	FAA Office of Environment and Energy
AEEC	Airlines Electronic Engineering Committee
AEG	Aircraft Evaluation Group
AEP	FAA Office of Aviation Policy Planning and Environment
AERA	Automated En-Route Air Traffic Control
AEX	Automated Execution
AF	Air Force
AF	Airway Facilities
AFB	Air Force Base
AFDSS	Air Fix Data Sub Set
AFER	Aircraft Fuel Expense Reconciliation System
AFIS	Automated Flight Inspection System
AFMS	Automatic Flight Management System
AFMT	Airway Facilities Management Team
AFO	Airport Field Office
AFP	Airspace Flow Program
AFP	Area Flight Plan
AFRES	Air Force Reserve Station
AFS	Airways Facilities Sector
AFS	Flight Standards Service
AFSFO	AFS Field Office
AFSFU	AFS Field Unit
AFSOU	AFS Field Office Unit (Standard is AFSFOU)
AFSS	Automated Flight Service Station
AFTIL	Airway Facilities Tower Integration Laboratory
AFTN	Automated Fixed Telecommunications Network
AFZ	Resource Management
AGC	FAA Office of the Chief Counsel
AGHME	Aircraft Geometric Height Measurement Element
AGI	FAA Office of Government and Industry Affairs
AGL	Above Ground Level
AGL	Alliance Great Lakes Region

AHR	FAA Office of Human Resources
AICS	Aircraft Inventory and Charter System
AID	Airport Information Desk
AIFSS	Automated International Flight Service
AIG	Airbus Industries Group
AILS	Automatic Instrument Landing System
AIM	Aeronautical Information Manual
AIM	Airman's Information Manual
AIP	Aeronautical Information Publication
AIP	Airport Improvement Plan
AIP	Airport Improvement Program
AIPA	Aeronautical Information Production Application
AIR	Aircraft Certification Service
AIRMET	Airmen's Meteorological Information
AIRNAV	Airports and Navigation Aids Database System
AIRNET	Airport Network Simulation Model
AIRPAC	Advisor for the Intelligent Resolution of Predicted Aircraft
AIS	Aeronautical Information Service
AIS	Aeronautical Information System
AIS	FAA Office of Information Systems Security
AIS	Aeronautical Information System
AIT	Automated Information Transfer
AITS	Automated Inventory Tracking System
AJA	Acquisition & Business Services, Air Traffic Organization
AJC	Communications Services, Air Traffic Organization
AJE	En Route & Oceanic Service, Air Traffic Organization
AJF	Finance Services, Air Traffic Organization
AJO	Chief Operating Officer, Air Traffic Organization
AJP	Operations Planning Services, Air Traffic Organization
AJR	System Operations Services, Air Traffic Organization
AJS	Safety Services, Air Traffic Organization
AJT	Terminal Service, Air Traffic Organization
AJW	Technical Operation Services, Air Traffic Organization
ALO	Aviation Logistics Organization
ALP	Airport Layout Plan
ALPA	Airlines Pilots Association

ALS	Approach Lighting System
ALSF	Approach Lighting System With Sequenced Flashing Lights
ALSF1	ALS with Sequenced Flashers I
ALSF2	ALS with Sequenced Flashers II
ALSIP	Approach Lighting System Improvement Plan
ALTRV	Altitude Reservation
AMASS	Airport Movement Area Safety System
AMC	Mike Monroney Aeronautical Center
AMCC	ACF/ARTCC Maintenance Control Center
AMCC	Air Route Traffic Control Center Maintenance Control Center
AMIC	Area Manager in Charge
AMIS	Aircraft Management Information System
AMOC	Alternative Methods of Compliance
AMOS	Automated Meteorological Observation Station
AMP	ARINC Message Processor (OR) Airport Master Plan
AMS	Acquisition Management System
AMT	Aviation Maintenance Technician
AMVER	Automated Mutual Assistance Vessel Rescue System
ANC	Alternate Network Connectivity
ANCA	Airport Noise and Capacity Act
AND	Associate Administrator for NAS Development
ANE	New England Region
ANG	Air National Guard
ANGB	Air National Guard Base
ANM	Northwest Mountain Region
ANMS	Automated Network Monitoring System
ANS	NAS Transition and Integration Directorate
ANS	NAS Transitions and Implementation
ANSI	American National Standards Institute
AO	Authorizing Official
AOA	Air Operations Area
AOA	FAA Office of the Administrator
AOAS	Advanced Oceanic Automation System
AOC	Airline Operational Control Center
AOC	FAA Office of Communications
AOCC	Atlantic Operations Control Center

AODR	Authorizing Official Designated Representative
AOP	NAS Operations
AOPA	Aircraft Owners and Pilots Association
AOS	Operational Support Service
AOV	Air Traffic Safety Oversight Service
AP	Acquisition Plan
APB	Acquisition Program Baselines
API	FAA Office of International Aviation
APM	Approach Path Monitor
APP	Approach
APS	Airport Planning Standard
APTS	Automated Personnel Tracking System
APTS	AVN (Aviation Systems Standards) Process Tracking System
AQAFO	Aeronautical Quality Assurance Field Office
AQS	FAA Office of Quality, Integration and Executive Services
ARA	Research and Acquisition
ARAC	Army Radar Approach Control (AAF)
ARAC	Aviation Rulemaking Advisory Committee
ARC	Administrator's Review Committee
ARC	Airlines Reporting Corporation
ARC	Aviation Review Committee
ARC	FAA Office of Regions and Center Operations
ARCTR	FAA Aeronautical Center or Academy
AREA	Automated En Route Air Traffic Control
ARF	Airport Reservation Function
ARFF	Aircraft Rescue and Fire Fighting
ARINC	Aeronautical Radio Incorporated
ARINC	Aeronautical Radio, Inc.
ARLNO	Airline Office
ARM	FAA Office of Rulemaking
ARO	Airport Reservation Office
ARP	Airport Reference Point
ARP	FAA Airports Organization
ARP	FAA Office of Airports
ARS	Air Traffic Requirements Service
ARS	Airport Surveillance Radar

ARS	Automated Reproduction System
ARSA	Airport Service Radar Area
ARSR	Air Route Surveillance Radar
ARSR	Long Range Surveillance Radar
ARTCC	Air Route Traffic Control Center
ARTS	Automated Radar Terminal System
ASAP	Aviation Safety Action Program
ASAS	Aviation Safety Analysis System
ASC	AUTODIN Switching Center
ASCP	Aviation System Capacity Plan
ASD	Aircraft Situation Display
ASDA	Accelerate Stop Distance Available
ASDE	Area Surveillance Detection Equipment - (Radar)
ASDE-X	Airport Surface Detection Equipment
ASH	FAA Office of Security & Hazardous Materials
ASI	Aviation Safety Inspector
ASIAS	Aviation Safety Information Analysis and Sharing
ASLAR	Aircraft Surge Launch And Recovery
ASM	Available Seat Mile
ASO	Southern Region
ASOS	Automated Surface Observing System
ASOS	Automated Surface Observing Systems
ASP	Arrival Sequencing Program
ASPM	Aviation System Performance Metrics
ASPM	Aviation System Performance Metrics
ASQP	Airline Service Quality Performance
ASR	Airport Surveillance Radar
ASR	Airways Facilities Spectrum Policy and Management
ASR	Alkali Silica Reactivity
ASR	Terminal Surveillance Radar
ASR-WSP	Airport Surveillance Radar-Weather System Processor
AST	FAA Office of Commercial Space Transportation
ASTA	Airport Surface Traffic Automation
ASV	Airline Schedule Vendor
ASW	Southwest Region
ASYNC	Asynchronous Concentrator

AT	Air Traffic
AT&T	American Telephone and Telegraph
AT&T	ASDC AT&T Agency Service Delivery Center
AT&T	CSA AT&T Customer Support Associate
ATA	Air Transport Association of America
ATA	Airline Transport Association
ATAS	Airspace and Traffic Advisory Service
ATC	Air Traffic Control
ATCA	Air Traffic Control Association
ATCAA	Air Traffic Control Assigned Airspace
ATCAA	ATC Assigned Airspace
ATCBI	Maintenance of Air Traffic Control Beacon Indicator
ATCCC	Air Traffic Control Command Center
ATCO	Air Taxi Commercial Operator
ATCOTS	Air Traffic Control Optimum Training Solutions
ATCRB	Air Traffic Control Radar Beacon
ATCRBS	Air Traffic Control Radar Beacon System
ATCS	Air Traffic Control Specialist
ATCSCC	Air Traffic Control Systems Command Center
ATCT	Airport Traffic Control Tower
ATIDS	Airport Surface Target Identification System
ATIS	Automated Terminal Information Service
ATIS	Automatic Terminal Information Service
ATIS	Automatic Terminal Information Service
ATISR	ATIS Recorder
ATM	Air Traffic Management
ATM	Air Traffic Manager
ATM	Asynchronous Transfer Mode
ATMAC	Air Traffic Management Advisory Committee
ATMS	Advanced Traffic Management System
ATMS	Automated Training Management System
ATN	Aeronautical Telecommunications Network
ATO	Air Traffic Organization
ATODN	AUTODIN Terminal (FUS)
ATOMS	Air Traffic Operations Management System
ATOP	Advanced Technologies and Oceanic Procedures

ATOS	Air Transportation Oversight System
ATOVN	AUOTVON (Facility)
ATR	Air Traffic Requirements
ATREP	Air Traffic Representative
ATS	Air Traffic Services
ATSAP	Air Traffic Safety Action Program
ATSCCP	ATS Contingency Command Post
ATSS	Airway Transportation Systems Specialist
ATTIS	AT&T Information Systems
AUTODIN	DoD Automatic Digital Network
AUTOVON	DoD Automatic Voice Network
AVN	Aviation Standards National Field Office, Oklahoma City
AVN	Aviation System Standards
AVON	AUTOVON Service
AVS	FAA Office of Aviation Safety
AVSI	Aerospace Vehicle Systems Institute
AWIS	Airport Weather Information
AWOS	Automated Weather Observing System
AWP	Aviation Weather Processor
AWP	Western Pacific Region
AWPG	Aviation Weather Products Generator
AWS	Air Weather Station
AWSS	Automated Weather Sensors System
AWTT	Aviation Weather Technology Transfer
AXX	One of the 9 Regional Offices
BA	Budget Analyst
BAD	Budget Analysis Database
BANS	BRITE Alphanumeric System
BART	Billing Analysis Reporting Tool (GSA software tool)
BASIC	Basic Contract Observing Station
BASOP	Military Base Operations
BCA	Benefit/Cost Analysis
BCR	Benefit/Cost Ratio
BDAT	Digitized Beacon Data
BERMS	Beacon Environmental Remote Monitoring Subsystem
BFO	Backfill Overtime

BFO	Blazing Flash of the Obvious (DOD)
BIM	Building Information Modeling
BIP	Backup Interface Processor
BMP	Best Management Practices
BOC	Bell Operating Company
BOD	Beneficial Occupancy Date
BPB	Business Plan Builder
BPS	Bits Per Second
BRI	Basic Rate Interface
BRITE	Bright Radar Indicator Terminal Equipment
BRITE	Bright Radar Indicator Tower Equipment
BRL	Building Restriction Line
BUEC	Back-up Emergency Communications
BUECE	Back-up Emergency Communications Equipment
C&A	Certification and Accreditation
C/S/S/N	Capacity/Safety/Security/Noise
CA	Conflict Alert
CAA	Civil Airworthiness Authority
CAA	Civil Aviation Authority
CAA	Clean Air Act
CAAFI	Commercial Aviation Alternative Fuels Initiative
CAASD	Center for Advanced Aviation System Development
CAB	Civil Aeronautics Board
CAD	Computer-aided Design
CAD	Computer-aided Drawing
CAD	Computer-aided Design
CAEG	Computer-aided Engineering Graphics
CAI	Contractor-Acceptance Inspection
CAIRS	Cable Assignment Information Retrieval System
CAMI	Civil Aerospace Medical Institute
CAP	Civil Air Patrol
CAR	Civil Aviation Regulations
CARAT	Center for Aviation Research and Aerospace Technology
CARF	Central Altitude Reservation Facility
CARF	Central Altitude Reservation Function
CARS	Civilian Air Routes System

CARSR	Common Air Route Surveillance Radar
CARTS	Common Automated Radar Terminal System
CAS	Cost Accounting System
CASA	Controller Automated Spacing Aid
CASFO	Civil Aviation Security Office
CASS	Continuing Analysis and Surveillance System
CASST	Commercial Aviation Safety Strategic Team
CAST	Certification Authority Software Team
CASTLE	Consolidated Automated System for Time and Labor Entry
CAT	Category
CAT	Clear Air Turbulence
CATTS	Computerized Air Traffic Training System
CATX	Categorical Exclusion
CAU	Crypto Ancillary Unit
CBI	Computer Based Instruction
CC	Construction Coordinator
CC&O	Customer Cost and Obligation
CCC	Communications Command Center
CCCC	Staff Communications
CCCH	Central Computer Complex Host
CCS7-NI	Communication Channel Signal-7 Network Interconnect
CCSD	Command Communications Service Designator
CCU	Central Control Unit
CD	Common Digitizer
CD	Compact Disc
CD-ROM	Compact Disc Read-Only Memory
CDA	Continuous Descent Arrival
CDB	Corporate Database
CDC	Computer Display Channel
CDD	Corporate Data Dictionary
CDL	Configuration Deviation List
CDM	Collaborative Decision Making
CDR	Cost Detail Report
CDRA	Cooperative Research and Development Agreement
CDS	Central Dispatch System
CDT	Controlled Departure Time

CDTI	Cockpit Display of Traffic Information
CDV	Compressed Digital Video
CED	Categorical Exclusion Determination
CENRAP	Center Radar Arts Presentation
CENTX	Central Telephone Exchange
CEP	Capacity Enhancement Program
CEQ	Council on Environmental Quality
CERAP	Center Radar Approach Control
CERAP	Central Radar Approach
CFC	Central Flow Control
CFCF	Central Flow Control Facility
CFCS	Central Flow Control Service
CFI	Certified Flight Instructor
CFIT	Controlled Flight Into Terrain
CFR	Code of Federal Regulations
CFWP	Central Flow Weather Processor
CFWU	Central Flow Weather Unit
CG	Center of Gravity
CGAS	Coast Guard Air Station
CHI	Computer Human Interface
CIO	Chief Information Officer
CIP	Capital Investment Plan
CISO	Chief Information Security Officer
CIWS	Corridor Integrated Weather System
CLC	Course Line Computer
CLEEN	Continuous Lower Energy, Emissions & Noise
CLIN	Contract Line Item
CLT	Calculated Landing Time
CM	Configuration Management
CMAP	Center Mapping Automation Program
CMFO	Certificate Management Field Office
CMIS	Certificate Management Information System
CMO	Certificate Management Office
CMU	Certificate Management Unit
CNMPS	Canadian Minimum Navigation Performance Specification Airspace
CNS	Communications, Navigation and Surveillance

CNS	Consolidated NOTAM System
CNSP	Consolidated NOTAM System Processor
CO	Central Office
CO	Contracting Officer
COE	Center of Excellence
COE	U.S. Army Corps of Engineers
COMCO	Command Communications Outlet
CONOPS	Concept of Operations
CONUS	Continental United States
COOP	Continuity of Operations Plan
CORP	Private Corporation other than ARINC or MITRE
COTR	Contracting Officer's Technical Representative
COTR	Contracting Officer's Technical Representative
COTS	Commercial Off-the-Shelf
CP	Conflict Probe
CPC	Certified Professional Controller
CPCS	Consolidated Production Control System
CPDLC	Controller Pilot Data Link Communications
CPE	Customer Premise Equipment
CPIC	Capital Planning and Investment Control
CPMIS	Consolidated Personnel Management Information System
CRA	Conflict Resolution Advisory
CRC	Coordinating Research Council
CRDA	Converging Runway Display Aid
CRDA	Cooperative Research & Development Agreement
CRM	Crew Resource Management
CRT	Cathode Ray Tube
CSA	Central Service Area
CSA	Communications Service Authorization
CSA	Comparative Safety Assessment
CSA	Central Service Area
CSAP	Combined Services Access Point
CSAP	Common Services Access Point
CSC	Central Service Center
CSC	Central Service Center
CSER	Contractor Site Engineering Report

CSIS	Centralized Storm Information System
CSMC	Cyber Security Management Center
CSO	Customer Service Office
CSR	Communications Service Request
CSS	Central Site System
CSTA	Chief Scientist and Technical Advisor
CSTWRK	Cost Work
CTA	Control Area
CTA	Controlled Time of Arrival
CTA/FIR	Control Area/Flight Information Region
CTAF	Common Traffic Advisory Frequency
CTAS	Center TRACON Automation System
CTMA	Center Traffic Management Advisor
CUPS	Consolidated Uniform Payroll System
CVFR	Controlled Visual Flight Rules
CVTS	Compressed Video Transmission Service
CW	Continuous Wave
CWO	Contract Weather Observer
CWP	Central Weather Processor
CWP	Corporate Work Plan
CWSU	Central Weather Service Unit
CWY	Clearway
D-ATIS	Digital - Automatic Terminal Information Service
DA	Decision Altitude/Decision Height
DA	Descent Advisor
DA	Direct Access
DA/H	Decision Altitude/Height
DABBS	DITCO Automated Bulletin Board System
DACS	Digital Aeronautical Chart Supplement
DADS	Digital Aeronautical Database System
DAFIS	Departmental Accounting and Financial Information System
DAIR	Direct Altitude and Identity Readout
DALR	Digital Audio Legal Recorder
DAR	Designated Agency Representative
DARC	Direct Access Radar Channel
DARP	Dynamic Aircraft Route Planning

DASI	Digital Altimeter Setting Indicator
DASR	Digital Airport Surveillance Radar
DB	Database
dB	Decibel
DBA	Database Administrator
dBA	Decibels A-Weighted
DBCRC	Defense Base Closure and Realignment Commission
DBE	Disadvantaged Business Enterprise
DBMS	Data Base Management System
DBRITE	Digital Bright Radar Indicator Tower Equipment
DCA	Defense Communications Agency
DCAA	Dual Call, Automatic Answer Device
DCC	Direct Channel Complex
DCCU	Data Communications Control Unit
DCE	Data Communications Equipment
DDA	Dedicated Digital Access
DDD	Direct Distance Dialing
DDM	Difference in Depth of Modulation
DDS	Digital Data Service
DEA	Drug Enforcement Agency
DEDS	Data Entry and Display System
DEIS	Draft Environmental Impact Statement
DEM	Digital Elevation Model
DEP	Departure
DEWIZ	Distance Early Warning Identification Zone
DF	Direction Finder
DFAX	Digital Facsimile
DFI	Direction Finding Indicator
DFL	Daily Flight Log
DFM	Departure Flow Management
DGNSS	Differential Global Navigation Satellite System
DGPS	Differential Global Positioning Satellite (System)
DGPS	Differential Global Positioning System
DH	Decision Height
DHS	Department of Homeland Security
DIA	Denver International Airport

DID	Direct Inward Dial
DIP	Drop and Insert Point
DIRF	Direction Finding
DISU	Drug Investigation Support Unit
DITCO	Defense Information Technology Contracting Office Agency
DLAP	Data Link Applications Processor
DLRS	Digital Legal Recording System
DME	Distance Measuring Equipment
DME/P	Precision Distance Measuring Equipment
DMN	Data Multiplexing Network
DMRS	Database Management Reporting System
DMS	Data Management System
DMS	Drawing Management System
DNL	Day-Night Equivalent Sound Level
DOD	Department of Defense
DOD	Direct Outward Dial
DOF	Digital Obstacle File
DOI	Department of Interior
DOS	Department of State
DOT	Department of Transportation
DOTCC	Department of Transportation Computer Center
DOTS	Dynamic Ocean Track System
DOTS	Dynamic Ocean Tracking System
DOVE	DSR Oceanic VSCS En Route Implementation Working Group
DP	Departure Procedures
DPE	Designated Pilot Examiner
DR	Disaster Recovery
DRP	Disaster Recovery Plan
DSCS	Digital Satellite Compression Service
DSG	Data Services Group
DSP	Departure Sequencing Program
DSR	Display System Replacement
DSS	Decision Support System
DSUA	Dynamic Special Use Airspace
DTED	Digital Terrain Elevation Data
DTM	Digital Terrain Model

DTS	Dedicated Transmission Service
DUAT	Direct User Access Terminal
DUATS	Direct User Access Terminal System
DVD	Digital Versatile Disk
DVFR	Day Visual Flight Rules
DVFR	Defense Visual Flight Rules
DVOF	Digital Vertical Obstruction File
DVOR	Doppler Very High Frequency Omni Directional Range
DVOR	Doppler Very High Frequency Omni-- Directional Range
DVRS	Digital Voice Recorder System
DYSIM	Dynamic Simulator
E-MSAW	En Route Automated Minimum Safe Altitude Warning
EA	Enterprise Architecture
EA	Environmental Assessment
EARS	En Route Analysis and Reporting System
EARTS	En Route Automated Radar Tracking System
EASA	European Aviation Safety Agency
EBC	Event Based Currency
EBUS	Enhanced Backup Surveillance
EC	Engineering Center
ECG	En Route Communications Gateway
ECOM	En Route Communications
eCPIC	Electronic Capital Planning Investment Control
ECVFP	Expanded Charted Visual Flight Procedures
EDC	Early Display Configuration
EDC	En Route Departure Capability
EDC	Enterprise Data Center
EDCT	Estimated Departure Control Time
EDCT	Expedite Departure Path
EDDA	Environmental Due Diligence Audit
EDI	Electronic Data Interchange
EDMS	Electronic Document Management Systems
EDMS	Emissions and Dispersion Modeling System
EDS	Enterprise Database System
EEO	Equal Employment Opportunity
EFAS	En Route Flight Advisory Service

EFB	Electronic Flight Bag
EFC	Expect Further Clearance
EFIS	Electronic Flight Information Systems
EFSTS	Electronic Flight Strip Transfer System
EIAF	Expanded Inward Access Features
EIS	Environmental Impact Statement
ELD	Electrical Load Database
eLMS	Electronic Learning Management System
ELT	Emergency Locator Transmitter
ELWRT	Electrowriter
EMAS	Engineered Materials Arresting System
EMPS	En Route Maintenance Processor System
EMS	Environmental Management System
ENAV	En Route Navigational Aids
EOF	Emergency Operating Facility
eOPF	Electronic Official Personnel File
EOSH	Environmental and Occupational Safety & Health
EOSH	Environmental Compliance Occupational Safety and Health
EPA	Environmental Protection Agency
EPI	Element Performance Inspection
EPS	Engineered Performance Standards
EPSS	Enhanced Packet Switched Service
ERAD	En Route Broadband Radar
ERAM	En Route Automation Modernization
ERIDS	En Route Information Display System
ERIT	Enhanced Radar Intelligent Tool
ERM	En Route Spacing Program
ERMS	Environmental Remote Monitoring System
ES&H	Environmental Safety and Health
ESA	Eastern Service Area
ESC	Eastern Service Center
ESC	Enterprise Service Center
ESC	Eastern Service Center
ESEC	En Route Broadband Secondary Radar
ESF	Extended Superframe Format
ESIS	Enhanced Status Information System

ESIS	Environmental Safety Information System
ESP	En Route Spacing Program
ESP	En Route Sequencing Program
ESRI	Environmental Systems Research Institute
ESYS	En Route Equipment Systems
ETA	Estimated Time of Arrival
ETE	Estimated Time En Route
ETG	Enhanced Target Generator
ETMS	Enhanced Traffic management Systems
ETN	Electronic Telecommunications Network
ETO	Engineering Technical Officer
ETVCT	En Route Training Voice Communication Tool
ETVS	Enhanced Terminal Voice Switch
EUROCAE	European Organization for Civil Aviation Equipment
EVAS	Enhanced Vortex Advisory System
EVCS	Emergency Voice Communications System
EVFR	Electronic Visual Flight Rules
EVM	Earned Value Management
F&E	Facilities and Equipment
FAA	Federal Aviation Administration
FAAAC	FAA Aeronautical Center
FAACIS	FAA Communications Information System
FAASTeam	FAA Safety Team
FAATC	FAA Technical Center
FAATC	Federal Aviation Administration Technical Center
FAATSAT	FAA Telecommunications Satellite
FAATSAT	Federal Aviation Administration Telecommunications Satellite
FAC	Facility
FACUTL	Facility Utilization System
FADE	FAA/Airline Data Exchange
FAF	Final Approach Fix
FAIRS	Federal Aircraft Management Information System
FAMIS	Federal Air Marshal Information System
FANS	Future Air Navigation System
FAP	Final Approach Point
FAPM	FTS2000 Associate Program Manager

FAQ	Frequently Asked Questions
FAR	Federal Aviation Regulation
FARM	Fielded Automation Requirements Management
FASC	FAA Aviation Safety Center
FAST	Final Approach Spacing Tool
FAX	Facsimile Equipment
FBO	Fixed Base Operator
FBS	Fall Back Switch
FCC	Federal Communications Commission
FCLT	Freeze Calculated Landing Time
FCM	Flight Schedule Monitor
FCOM	FSS Radio Voice Communications
FCPU	Facility Central Processing Unit
FCT	Federal Contract Tower
FDAT	Flight Data
FDAT	Flight Data Entry and Printout (FDEP) and Flight Data Service
FDE	Flight Data Entry
FDEP	Flight Data Entry and Printout
FDIO	Flight Data Input/Output
FDIOC	Flight Data Input/Output Center
FDIOR	Flight Data Input/Output Remote
FDM	Frequency Division Multiplexing
FDMSAW	Fully Digital Minimum Safe Altitude Warning
FDP	Flight Data Processing
FDP/RDP	Flight Data Processing/Radar Data Processing
FDR	Federal Data Registry
FDT	Flight Deck Training Program
FED	Federal
FEIS	Final Environmental Impact Statement
FEODP	Flight Edit and On-Demand Printing
FEP	Front End Processor
FERS	Facility and Equipment Reporting System
FFAC	From Facility
FFLA	Flexible Flight Level Assignment
FFRDC	Federal Funded Research & Development Center
FIAO	Flight Inspection Area Office

FICO	Flight Inspection Central Office
FIFO	Flight Inspection Field Office
FIG	Flight Inspection Group
FINO	Flight Inspection National Field Office
FIO	Flight Inspection Office
FIP	Facility Improvement Program
FIPS	Federal Information Publication Standard
FIR	Flight Information Region
FIRE	Fire Station
FIRMR	Federal Information Resource Management Regulation
FIRPS	Flight Inspection Reports Processing System
FIS	Flight Information Services
FISDL	Flight Information Services Data Link
FISMA	Federal Information Security Management Act of 2002
FISMA	Federal Information Security Management Act of 2002
FITS	FAA/Industry Training Standards
FL	Flight Level
FLDS	Flight Loads Data System
FLIP	Flight Information Publication
FLM	Front Line Manager
FLOWSIM	Traffic Flow Planning Simulation
FLSA	Fair Labor Standards Act
FLTCK	Flight Check
FMA	Final Monitor Aid
FMC	Frontline Managers Courses
FMF	Facility Master File
FMIS	FTS2000 Management Information System
FMO	Facility Management Office
FMP	Field Maintenance Party
FMS	Financial Management System
FMS	Flight Management System
FNMS	FTS2000 Network Management System
FOD	Foreign Object Damage
FOIA	Freedom of Information Act
FOMS	Flight Operations Management System
FONSI	Finding of No Significant Impact

FOQA	Flight Operations Quality Assurance
FOTS	Fiber Optics Transmission System
FOUO	For Official Use Only
FP	Flight Plan
FPI	Fluorescent Penetrate Inspection
FPL	Full Performance Level
FPO	Flight Procedures Office
FPPS	Federal Personnel Payroll System
FPS	Military Primary Radar
FRC	Request Full Route Clearance
FRD	Facility Reference Data
FRMS	Facility Roster Management System
FS	Flight Standards
FSAS	Flight Service Automation System
FSCAP	Flight Safety Critical Aircraft Parts
FSDO	Flight Standards District Office
FSDPS	Flight Service Data Processing System
FSEP	Facility, Service, and Equipment Profile
FSFO	Flight Standards Field Office
FSIAG	Flight Service Information Area Group
FSM	Flight Schedule Monitor
FSP	Flight Strip Printer
FSPD	Freeze Speed Parameter
FSRM	Facility Security Risk Management
FSS	Flight Service Station
FSSA	Flight Service Station Automated Service
FST	Fuel Storage Tanks
FSTS	Federal Secure Telephone Service
FSYS	Flight Service Station Equipment Systems
FTE	Full Time Equivalent
FTI	FAA Telecommunications Infrastructure
FTP	File Transfer Protocol
FTS	Federal Telecommunications System
FTS2000	Federal Telecommunications System 2000
FUS	Functional Units or Systems
FWCS	Flight Watch Control Station

FWS	FAA Weather Service
FY	Fiscal Year
GA	General Aviation
GAA	General Aviation Activity
GAAA	General Aviation Activity and Avionics
GADO	General Aviation District Office
GAO	Government Accountability Office
GAO	Government Accounting Office
GCA	Ground Control Approach
GDE	Ground Delay Enhancements
GDP	Ground Delay Program
GENOT	General Notice
GETS	Government Emergency Telecommunications Service
GETS	Grievance Electronic Tracking System
GFE	Government Furnished Equipment
GFM	Government Furnished Materials
GFP	Government Furnished Property
GIS	Geographic Information System
GLONASS	Global Orbiting Navigational Satellite System
GMCC	General National Airspace System Maintenance Control Center
GML	Geography Markup Language
GMS	Grants Management System
GNAS	General National Airspace System
GNSS	Global Navigation Satellite System
GOES	Geostationary Operational Environmental Satellite
GOESF	GOES Feed Point
GOEST	GOES Terminal Equipment
GOMP	Gulf of Mexico Program
GPO	Government Printing Office
GPRA	Government Performance and Results Act
GPS	Global Positioning Satellite
GPS	Global Positioning System
GPWS	Ground Proximity Warning System
GRADE	Graphical Airspace Design Environment
GS	Glide Slope
GS	Glide Slope Indicator

GSA	General Services Administration
GSE	Ground Support Equipment
GTM	General Terrain Model
GUI	Graphic User Interface
GWDS	Graphic Weather Display System
HAA	Height Above Airport
HAL	Height Above Landing
HARS	High Altitude Route System
HAT	Height Above Touchdown
HAZMAT	Hazardous Materials
HCAP	High Capacity Carriers
HCS	Host Computer System
HDME	NDB with Distance Measuring Equipment
HDQ	FAA Headquarters
HDR	Hardware Discrepancy Report
HELI	Heliport
HEMS	Helicopter Emergency Medical Service
HF	High Frequency
HI-EFAS	High Altitude EFAS
HID	Host Interface Display
HID/NAS/LAN	Host Interface Device/National Airspace System/Local Area Network
HIRL	High Intensity Runway Lights
HLDC	High Level Data Link Control
HMI	Hazardously Misleading Information
HOV	High Occupancy Vehicle
HQ	FAA Headquarters
HSI	Horizontal Situation Indicators
HSPD	Homeland Security Presidential Directive
HUD	Heads Up Display
HUD	Housing and Urban Development
HUMS	Health & Usage Monitoring Systems
HVAC	Heating, Ventilating, and Air Conditioning
HWAS	Hazardous In-Flight Weather Advisory
Hz	Hertz
I&I	Impact and Implementation
I/AFSS	International AFSS

IA	Indirect Access
IA	Information Assurance
IAF	Initial Approach Fix
IAP	Instrument Approach Procedures
IAPA	Instrument Approach Procedures Automation
IAR	Investment Analysis Report
IAS	Investment Analysis Staff
IAT	Investment Analysis Team
IATA	International Air Transport Association
IBM	International Business Machines
IBP	International Boundary Point
IBR	Intermediate Bit Rate
IC	Implementation Center
ICAO	International Civil Aviation Organization
iCMM	integrated Capability Maturity Model
ICMS	Integrated Control and Monitor System
ICSS	Integrated Communications Switching System
ICSS	International Communications Switching Systems
ID	Identification
IDAT	Interfacility Data
IDP	Individual Development Plan
IDS	Intrusion Detection System
IF	Intermediate Fix
IFB	Invitation For Bid
IFCP	Interfacility Communications Processor
IFDS	Interfacility Data System
IFEA	In-Flight Emergency Assistance
IFO	International Field Office
IFP	Instrument Flight Procedures
IFPA	Instrument Flight Procedures Automation Program
IFR	Instrument Flight Rules
IFSS	International Flight Service Station
IG	Inspector General
IGIA	Interagency Group on International Aviation
IIE	Integrated Information Environment
ILM	Inventory Logistics and Maintenance Suite

ILS	Instrument Landing System
ILSP	Integrated Logistics Support Plan
IM	Inner Marker
IMC	Instrument Meteorological Conditions
INM	Integrated Noise Model
INS	Inertial Navigation System
IOC	Initial Operating Capability
IOC	Initial Operating Condition
IOT&E	Independent Operational Test and Evaluation
IP	Internet Protocol
IPDS	Instrument Procedure Development System
IPMS	IT Program Management System
IPR	In Process Review
IPT	Integrated Product Team
iRCAS	Intranet Radio Coverage Analysis System
IRD	Initial Requirements Document
IRM	Information Resource Management
IRMC	Integrated Risk Management Checklist
IRMP	Information Resources Management Plan
ISBP	Information Security Business Portal
ISC	Initial System Capability
ISDN	Integrated Services Digital Network
ISMLS	Interim Standard Microwave Landing System
ISO	Information System Owner
ISS	Information Systems Security
ISSCA	Information Systems Security Certification Agent
ISSM	Information Systems Security Manager
ISSO	Information Systems Security Officer
IST	InterService Team
IT	Information Technology
ITC	In-Trail Climb
ITD	In-Trail Descent
ITEB	Information Technology Executive Board
ITI	Interactive Terminal Interface
ITIL	Information Technology Infrastructure Library
ITMRA	Information Technology Management Reform Act

ITSM	Information Technology Service Management
ITWS	Integrated Terminal Weather System
IVRS	Interim Voice Response System
IVSR	Interim Voice Switch Replacement Program
IVT	Interactive Video Teletraining
IW	Inside Wiring
IWGDS	Interim Weather Graphic-Display System
J2EE	Java 2 Enterprise Edition
JAI	Joint Acceptance Inspection
JCN	Job Control Number
JPDO	Joint Planning and Development Office
JRC	Joint Resources Council
JSS	Joint Surveillance System
Kbps	Kilobits Per Second
KCAS	Knots Calibrated Airspeed
kHz	Kilohertz
KIAS	Knots Indicated Airspeed
KSN	Knowledge Services Network
KVDT	Keyboard Video Display Terminal
Kbps	Kilobits Per Second
KCAS	Knots Calibrated Airspeed
kHz	Kilohertz
KIAS	Knots Indicated Airspeed
KSN	Knowledge Services Network
KVDT	Keyboard Video Display Terminal
LAA	Local Airport Advisory
LAAS	Local Area Augmentation System
LAAS	Low Altitude Alert System
LABS	Leased A B Service
LABS	Los Angeles Basin Study
LABSC	LABS GS-200 Computer
LABSR	LABS Remote Equipment
LABSW	LABS Switch System
LAC	Logical Access Control
LAGPS	Local Area Global Positioning System
LAHSO	Land and Hold Short Operation

LAN	Local Area Network
LATA	Local Access and Transport Area
LAWRS	Limited Aviation Weather Reporting Service
LAWRS	Limited Aviation Weather Reporting System
LBR	LAN Based Random Access Plan Position Indicator
LBR	LAN Based Random Access Plan Position Indicator
LCC	Life Cycle Cost
LCF	Local Control Facility
LCGS	Low Cost Ground Surveillance Radar
LCN	Local Communications Network
LDA	Landing Directional Aid
LDA	Localizer Directional Aid
LDAP	Lightweight Directory Access Protocol
LDIN	Lead-In Lights
LDR	Labor Distribution Reporting
LEC	Local Exchange Carrier
LF	Low Frequency
LFDS	Large Facility Demarcation System
LFME	Local Flow Management Enhancements
LINCS	Leased Interfacility NAS Communications System
LIRL	Low Intensity Runway Lights
LIS	Logistics and Inventory System
LLWAS	Low Level Wind Shear Alert System
LM/MS	Low/Medium Frequency
LMM	Locator Middle Marker
LMS	Logistics Management Specialist
LMS	LORAN Monitor Site
LOA	Letter of Agreement
LOB	Line Of Business
LOC	Localizer
LOCID	Location Identifier
LOI	Letter of Intent
LOM	Compass Locator at Outer Marker
LOM	Locator Outer Marker
LORAN	Long-Range Aid to Navigation
LOV	List of Values

LPC	Logistics Program Coordinator
LPV	Lateral Precision Performance with Vertical Guidance
LPV	Localizer Performance with Vertical Guidance
LRCO	Limited Remote Communications Outlet
LRNAV	Long Range Navigation
LRR	Long Range Radar
LRRAP	Long Range Resource Allocation Plan
LSMS	Line Station Maintenance Section
M1FC	Model 1 Full Capacity
MAA	Maximum Authorized Altitude
MAC	Maintenance Action Code
MAC	Mean Aerodynamic Cord
MALS	Medium-Intensity Approach Lighting System
MALSF	Medium-Intensuty Approach Light System with Sequenced Flashers
MALSR	MALS with Runway Alignment Indicator Lights
MALSR	Medium-Intensity Approach Lighting System With Runway Alignment Indicator
MAM	Maintenance Assumed Monitoring
MAP	Maintenance Automation Program
MAP	Military Airport Program
MAP	Missed Approach Point
MAP	Missed Approach Procedure
MAP	Modified Access Pricing
MARSA	Military Assumes Responsibility for Separation
MASS	Maintenance Automation System Software
MBO	Management by Objectives
Mbps	Megabits Per Second
MBT	Maneuvers Based Training
MCA	Minimum Crossing Altitude
MCAS	Marine Corps Air Station
MCC	Maintenance Control Center
MCI	Mode C Intruder
MCK	Maintenance Check
MCL	Middle Compass Locater
MCS	Maintenance and Control System
MDA	Minimum Descent Altitude
MDCRS	Metereological Data Collection and Reporting System

MDFM	Material Delivery Forecast Module
MDT	Maintenance Data Terminal
MEA	Minimum Enroute Altitude
MEARTS	Micro-EARTS
MEL	Minimum Equipment List
METAR	Aviation Routine Weather Report
METI	Meteorological Information
MF	Middle Frequency
MFJ	Modified Final Judgment
MFO	Medical Field Office
MFT	Meter Fix Crossing Time/Slot Time
MHA	Minimum Holding Altitude
MHz	Megahertz
MIA	Minimum IFR Altitudes
MIDO	Manufacturing Inspection District Office
MIO	Manufacturing Inspection Office
MIRL	Medium Intensity Runway Lights
MIS	Management Information System
MIS	Meteorological Impact Statement
MISC	Miscellaneous
MISO	Manufacturing Inspection Satellite Office
MIT	Miles In Trail
MLS	Microwave Landing System
MM	Middle Marker
MMAC	Mike Monroney Aeronautical Center
MMC	Maintenance Monitoring Console
MMPI	Minnesota Multiphase Personality Inventory
MMR	Multi-Mode Receiver
MMS	Maintenance Monitoring System
MNPS	Minimum Navigation Performance Specification
MNPSA	Minimum Navigation Performance Specifications Airspace
MNS	Mission Needs Statement
MOA	Memorandum of Agreement
MOA	Military Operations Area
MOC	Memorandum of Cooperation
MOCA	Minimum Obstruction Clearance Altitude

MOCC	Mid-States Operations Control Center
MOD	Memorandum of Decision
MODE C	Altitude Reporting Mode of Secondary Radar
MODE S	Mode Select; Discrete Addressable Secondary Radar System With Data Link
MODEM	Modulator-Demodulator
MOS	Military Operations Specialst
MOU	Memorandum of Understanding
MPAR	Multi-function Phased Array Radar
MPO	Metropolitan Planning Organization
MPS	Maintenance Processor Subsystem (OR) Master Plan Supplement
MRA	Minimum Reception Altitude
MRC	Monthly Recurring Charge
MRM	Maintenance Returned Monitoring
MSA	Minimum Safe Altitude
MSAW	Minimum Safe Altitude Warning
MSD	Multi-Site Damage
MSDA	Material Safety Data Sheet
MSDS	Microsoft Data Engine
MSL	Mean Sea Level
MSN	Message Switching Network
MSR	Monthly Status Report
MTCS	Modular Terminal Communications System
MTD	Moving Target Detection
MTI	Moving Target Indicator
MTR	Military Training Route
MUX	Multiplexor
MVA	Minimum Vectoring Altitude
MVFR	Marginal Visual Flight Rules
MWP	Meteorological Weather Processor
N/A	Not Applicable
NAAQS	National Ambient Air Quality Standards
NACG	National Aeronautical Charting Group
NADA	NADIN Concentrator
NADIN	National Airspace Data Interchange Network
NADSW	NADIN Switches
NAILS	National Airspace Integrated Logistics Support

NAMS	NADIN IA
NAP	Needs Assessment Program
NAPM	National Associate Program Manager
NAPRS	National Airspace Performance Reporting System
NAR	National Airspace Review 66
NARACS	National Radio Communications System
NARP	National Aviation Research Plan
NAS	National Air Space
NAS	National Airspace System
NAS	National Airspace System or Naval Air Station
NASDC	National Aviation Safety Data
NASE	NAS Adaptation Services Environment
NASP	National Airspace System Plan
NASPAC	National Airspace System Performance Analysis Capability
NASR	National Airspace System Resources
NASTEP	National Airspace System Technical Evaluation Program
NATCA	National Air Traffic Control Association
NATCA	National Air Traffic Controllers Association
NATCO	National Communications Switching Center
NATS	National Air Traffic Service
NAVAID	Navigation Aid
NAVAIDS	Navigational Aids
NAVMN	Navigation Monitor and Control
NAWAU	National Aviation Weather Advisory Unit
NAWPF	National Aviation Weather Processing Facility
NBAA	National Business Aircraft Association
NBCAP	National Beacon Code Allocation Plan
NBCFAE	National Black Coalition of Federal Aviation Employees
NCAR	National Center for Atmospheric Research; Boulder, CO
NCF	National Control Facility
NCIU	NEXRAD Communications Interface Unit
NCP	NAS Change Proposal
NCP	Noise Compatibility Program
NCS	National Communications System
NSD	Navigation System Database
NDB	Non-directional Beacon

NDC	National Data Center
NDI	Nondestructive Inspection
NDNB	NADIN II
NDP	National Airspace System Defense Programs
NEC	National Electric Code
NED	National Elevation Data
NEM	Noise Exposure Map
NEMC	Network Enterprise Maintenance Center
NEPA	National Environmental Policy Act
NEXRAD	Next Generation Weather Radar
NextGen	Next Generation Air Transportation System
NFAX	National Facsimile Service
NFD	National Flight Database
NFDC	National Flight Data Center
NFDD	National Flight Data Digest
NFIS	NAS Facilities Information System
NFP	NIMS Premier Facility
NGA	National Geospatial-Intelligence Agency
NHCFAE	National Hispanic Coalition of Federal Aviation Employees
NI	Network Interface
NICS	National Airspace System Interfacility Communications System
NICS	National Interfacility Communications System
NIMA	National Imagery and Mapping Agency
NIMS	NAS Infrastructure Management System
NIPT	National Infrastructure Planning Team
NISC	NAS Implementation Support Contract
NISC	NAS Integration Support Contractor
NIST	National Institute of Standards and Technologies
NM	Nautical Mile
NMAC	Near Mid Air Collision
NMC	National Meteorological Center
NMCE	Network Monitoring and Control Equipment
NMCS	Network Monitoring and Control System
NOAA	National Oceanic and Atmospheric Administration
NOC	Notice Of Completion
NOCC	National Operation Control Center

NOG	National Operations Group
NOM	NAS Operations Manager
NOREP	National Oceanic Review and Enhancement Program
NOTAM	Notice to Airmen
NPDES	National Pollutant Discharge Elimination System
NPE	Non-primary Airport Entitlement
NPIAS	National Plan for Integrated Airport Systems
NPM	NAS Program Manager/Management
NPR	National Performance Review
NPRM	Notice of Proposed Rulemaking
NRC	Non-Recurring Charge
NRCS	National Radio Communications Systems
NRP	National Route Program
NSAP	National Service Assurance Plan
NSC	National Service Center
NSP	National Simulator Program
NSRCATN	National Strategy to Reduce Congestion on America's Transportation Network
NSSFC	National Severe Storms Forecast Center
NSSL	National Severe Storms Laboratory; Norman, OK
NSWRH	NWS Regional Headquarters
NTAP	Notices To Airmen Publication
NTP	National Transportation Policy
NTP	Notice to Proceed
NTS	NOTAM Tracking System
NTSB	National Transportation Safety Board
NTZ	No Transgression Zone
NWP	National Work Plan
NWP	NextGen Weather Processor
NWS	National Weather Service
NWSR	NWS Weather Excluding NXRD
NXRD	Advanced Weather Radar System
O&M	Operations and Maintenance
O21	Ocean21
OAG	Official Airline Guide
OALT	Operational Acceptable Level of Traffic
OAMP	Off-Line Aircraft Management Program

OAP	Oceanic Automation Program
OAS	Oceanic Automation System
OASIS	Operational and Supportability Implementation System
OATS	Office Automation Technology Services
OAW	Off-airway Weather Station
OC4J	Oracle Containers for Java Enterprise Edition
OCA	Oceanic Control Area
OCC	Operations Control Center
OCDB	Oracle Content Database
ODAL	Omnidirectional Approach Lighting System
ODALS	Omnidirectional Approach Lighting Systems
ODAPS	Oceanic Display and Planning System
ODAPS	Oceanic Display and Processing Station
ODL	Oceanic Data Link
ODRA	Office of Dispute Resolution for Acquisition
ODS	Operational Data Store
OE	Obstacle Evaluation
OE/AAA	Obstruction Evaluation/Airport Airspace Analysis
OEM	Original Equipment Manufacturer
OEP	Operational Evolution Plan
OEP	Operational Evolution Plan/Partnership
OETS	Obstacle Evaluation Tracking System
OFA	Object Free Area
OFDPS	Offshore Flight Data Processing System
OFT	Outer Fix Time
OFZ	Obstacle Free Zone
OGC	Open Geospatial Consortium
OIG	Office of the Inspector General
OM	Outer Marker
OMB	Office of Management and Budget
OMEGA	Very Low Radio Navigation System
OMIC	Operations Manager in Charge
ONER	Oceanic Navigational Error Report
OPD	Optimum Profile Descent
OPI	Office of Primary Interest
OPLT	Operational Acceptable Level of Traffic

OPR	Office of Primary Responsibility
OPS	AF Operations
OPS	Operations
OPSNET	Operations Network
OPSW	Operational Switch
OPX	Off Premises Exchange
ORD	Operational Readiness Demonstration
ORD	Operational Readiness Demonstration - Milestone
ORS	Obstruction Repository System
OS	Operating System
OS	Operational Shakedown & Cutover
OSA	Operational Safety Assessment
OSD	Operational Suitability Demonstration
OSDS	Oceanic System Development and Support
OSHA	Occupational Safety and Health Administration
OSIP	Office Safety Inspection Program
OSRWG	Oceanic Separation Reduction Working Group
OST	Office of the Secretary of Transportation
OT&E	Operational Test and Evaluation
OTFO	Operations Technical Field Office
OTPS	Oceanic Traffic Planning System
OTR	Oceanic Transition Route
OTS	Organized Track System
OTS	Out of Service
P2R2	Preferred Route Reduction Program
PA	Project Authorization
PABX	Private Automated Branch Exchange
PAD	Packet Assembler/Disassembler
PAM	Peripheral Adapter Module
PAMRI	Peripheral Adapter Module Replacement Item
PANS	Procedures for Air Navigation Services
PAPI	Precision Approach Path Indicator
PAR	Precision Approach Radar
PAR	Preferential Arrival Route
PAS	Project Assignment Sheet
PASS	Professional Airway System Specialists

PATS	Precision Approach Tracking System
PATWAS	Pilots Automatic Telephone Weather Answering Service
PBCT	Proposed Boundary Crossing Time
PBRF	Pilot Briefing
PBX	Private Branch Exchange
PCA	Positive Control Airspace
PCB	Personnel Compensation and Benefits
PCB&T	Personnel Compensation Benefits and Travel
PCM	Pulse Code Modulation
PCN	Project Control Number
PCPS	Purchase Card Processing System
PCS	Permanent Change of Station
PCS	Power Conditioning System
PCS	Production Control System
PDA	Personal Digital Assistant
PDAR	Preferential Arrival And Departure Route
PDC	Pre-Departure Clearance
PDC	Program Designator Code
PDF	Portable Document Format
PDN	Public Data Network
PDR	Preferential Departure Route
PDS	Proficiency Development Specialists
PED	Personal Electronic Devices
PFAST	Passive Final Approach Spacing Tool
PFC	Passenger Facility Charge
PFC	Porous Friction Course
PgMM	Program Management Methodology
PGP	Planning Grant Program
PHA	Preliminary Hazard Analysis
PHL	Preliminary Hazard List
PIC	Principal Interexchange Carrier
PIDP	Programmable Indicator Data Processor
PII	Personally Identifiable Information
PIM	Program Implementation Manager
PIP	Primary Interface Processor
PIP	Program Implementation Plan

PIREP	Pilot Weather Report
PjMM	Project Management Methodology
PjSA	Project Scope Agreement
PKI	Public Key Infrastructure
PM	Preventive Maintenance
PMA	Parts Manufacturer Approval
PMC	Project Materials Cumulative
PML	Project Material List
PMS	Program Management System
POC	Point-of-Contact
POCC	Pacific Operations Control Center
POP	Point-Of-Presence
POT	Point-of-Termination
PPE	Personal Protective Equipment
PPIMS	Personal Property Information Management System
PPR	Personal Property Report
PR	Procurement Request
PR	Project Review/Program Review
PRI	Primary Rate Interface
PRM	Precision Runway Monitor
PSC	Program Support Center
PSD	Process Support Document
PSDN	Public Switched Data Network
PSL	Projected Service Life
PSN	Packet Switched Network
PSR	Project Status Report
PSS	Packet Switched Service
PSTN	Public Switched Telephone Network
PT	Product Team
PTC	Presumed-to-Conform
PTR	Program Technical/Trouble Report
PTS	Procedures Tracking System
PUB	Publication
PUP	Principal User Processor
PVC	Permanent Virtual Circuit
PVD	Plan View Display

PWI	Proximity Warning Indicator
QA	Quality Assurance
QAE	Quality Assurance Evaluator
QAR	Quality Assurance Resource
QC	Quality Control
QMS	Quality Management System
R&D	Research and Development
R,E&D	Research, Engineering and Development
RADLO	Regional Air Defense Liaison Office
RAIL	Runway Alignment Indicator Lights
RAPCO	Radar Approach Control (USAF)
RAPCON	Radar Approach Control
RAPCON	Radar Approach Control (FAA)
RAPPI	Random Access Plan Position Indicator
RASP	Regional Airport System Plan
RAT	Risk Assessment Team
RATCC	Radar Air Traffic Control Center
RATCF	Radar Air Traffic Control Facility (USN)
RBC	Rotating Beam Ceilometer
RBDPE	Radar Beacon Data Processing Equipment
RBPM	Remote Beacon Performance Monitor
RBSS	Radar Bomb Scoring Squadron
RCAG	Remote Communications Air/Ground
RCAS	Radio Coverage Analysis System
RCC	Rescue Coordination Center
RCCC	Regional Communications Control Center
RCE	Radio Control Equipment
RCF	Remote Communications Facility
RCIU	Remote Control Interface Unit
RCL	Radio Communications Link
RCLR	Radio Communications Link Repeater
RCLR	RCL Repeater
RCLT	RCL Terminal
RCM	Reliability Centered Maintenance
RCO	Remote Communications Outlet
RCU	Remote Control Unit

RD	Requirements Document
RDP	Radar Data Processing
RDSIM	Runway Delay Simulation Model
RDVS	Rapid Deployment Voice Switch
RE	Resident Engineer
REDAC	Research, Engineering & Development Advisory Committee
REDMACS	Research, Engineering, and Development Monitoring, Analysis and Control System
REGIS	Regional Information System
REIL	Runway End Identification Light
RF	Radio Frequency
RFI	Radio Frequency Interference
RFI	Request for Information
RFI	Return on Future Investment
RFQ	Request for Quotes
RIIEP	Runway Incursion Information Evaluation Program
RIP	Runway Incursion Program
RM	Risk Management
RMCC	Remote Monitor Control Center
RMCF	Remote Monitor Control Facility
RML	Radar Microwave Link
RMLR	RML Repeater
RMLS	Remote Monitoring and Logging System
RMLT	RML Terminal
RMM	Remote Maintenance Monitoring
RMMC	Remote Maintenance Monitoring and Control
RMMS	Remote Maintenance Monitoring System
RMMS	Remote Maintenance Monitoring Systems
RMS	Remote Maintenance Subsystem
RMS	Remote Monitoring Subsystem
RMS	Risk Management System
RMSC	Remote Monitoring Subsystem Concentrator
RMT	Resource Management Tool
RMT	Risk Management Team
RNAV	Area Navigation
RNP	Required Navigation Performance
RNP-10	Required Navigation Performance

ROA	Record of Assistance
ROC	Regional Operations Center
ROD	Record of Decision
ROM	Read-Only Memory
ROSA	Report of Service Activity
ROSHM	Regional Occupational Safety and Health Manager
ROT	Runway Occupancy Time
RP	Restoration Priority
RPC	Restoration Priority Code
RPG	Radar Processing Group
RPI	Real Property Inventory
RPM	Rational Portfolio Manager
RPM	RTP Program Manager
RPMES	Regional Program Manager for Environment and Safety
RPOC	Risk Point-of-Contact
RPR	Real Property Report
RPV	Remotely Piloted Vehicle
RPZ	Runway Protection Zone
RRCS	Remote Radio Control System
RRH	Remote Reading Hygrothermometer
RRHS	Remote Reading Hydrometer
RRWDS	Remote Radar Weather Display
RRWSS	RWDS Sensor Site
RSA	Runway Safety Area
RSAP	Runway Safety Action Plan
RSAT	Runway Safety Action Team
RSL	Runway Status Light
RSS	Remote Speaking System
RT	Remote Transmitter
RT&BTL	Radar Tracking and Beacon Tracking Level
RTAD	Remote Tower Alphanumeric Display
RTCA	Radio Technical Commission for Aeronautics
RTDS	Radar Terminal Display System
RTE	Route
RTP	Regional Transportation Plan
RTR	Remote Transmitter/Receiver

RTRD	Remote Tower Radar Display
RTS	Return to Service
RUC	Rapid Update Cycle
RVM	Radar Video Map
RVR	Runway Visual Range
RVSM	Reduced Vertical Separation Minima
RW	Runway
RWP	Real-time Weather Processor
RWSL	Runway Status Lights
RWY	Runway
RX	Receiver
S/S	Sector Suite
SA	System Administrator
SAC	Strategic Air Command
SAFI	Semi Automatic Flight Inspection
SAGA	System Safety Approach for General Aviation
SAI	Safety Attribute Inspection
SALS	Short Approach Lighting System
SAMS	Special Use Airspace Management System
SAN	Storage Area Network
SAPS	Staffing and Personnel System
SAR	Search and Rescue
SARP	Standards and Recommended Practices
SAS	Safety Assurance System
SASO	System Approach for Safety Oversight
SAT	Security, Awareness, and Training System
SAT	SEOAT Analytical Team
SATCOM	Satellite Communications
SAVES	Strategic Sourcing for the Acquisition of Various Equipment and Supplies
SAWRS	Supplemental Aviation Weather Reporting Service
SAWRS	Supplementary Aviation Weather Reporting System
SBGP	State Block Grant Program
SBIR	Small Business Innovation Research
SBS	Surveillance Broadcast Services
SBT	Scenario Based Training
SCADA	Supervisory Control and Data Acquisition

SCAP	System Certification and Accreditation Package
SCAT	Staffing and Cost Analysis Tool
SCC	System Command Center
SCT	Southern California Area TRACON (Metroplex)
SCVTS	Switched Compressed Video Telecommunications Service
SDF	Simplified Direction Finding
SDF	Software Defined Network
SDIS	Switched Digital Integrated Service
SDLC	Software Development Life Cycle
SDP	Service Delivery Point
SDR	Service Difficulty Report
SDR	System Documentation Release
SDS	Switched Data Service
SEC	Strategic Event Coordination
SECM	Safety and Environmental Compliance Manager
SECRA	Secondary Radar
SEL	Single Event Level
SELF	Simplified Short Approach Lighting System With Sequenced Flashing Lights
SEOAT	Systems Engineering Operational Analysis Team
SERC	Software Engineering Resource Center
SET	Spacing Efficiency Tool
SETA	System Engineering and Technical Assistance
SFAR	Special Federal Aviation Regulations
SFAR-38	Special Federal Aviation Regulation 38
SFD	Service Flow Diagram
SGI	Silicon Graphics Incorporated
SHPO	State Historic Preservation Officer
SHRP	Strategic Highway Research Program
SIAP	Standard Instrument Flight Procedure
SIC	Service Initiation Charge
SID	Standard Instrument Departure
SID	Station Identifier
SIGMET	Significant Meteorological Information
SIMMOD	Airspace and Airport Simulation Model
SIP	State Implementation Plan
SIR	Screening Information Request

SLEP	Service Life Extension Program
SM	Statute Mile
SMA	Surface Monitor Aid
SMA	Surface Movement Advisor
SMF	Systems Management Facility
SMGC	Surface Movement Guidance and Control
SMGCS	Surface Movement Guidance and Control System
SMMC	System Maintenance Monitor Console
SMO	System Management Office
SMPS	Sector Maintenance Processor Subsystem
SMS	Safety Management System
SMS	Simulation Modeling System
SMT	Schedule Management Toolset
SNR	Signal-to-Noise Ratio
SNT	Staffed NextGen Tower
SOAR	System of Airports Reporting
SOC	Service Operations Center
SOC	Service Oversight Center
SOIR	Simultaneous Operations On Intersecting Runways
SOIWR	Simultaneous Operations on Intersecting Wet Runways
SOP	Standard Operating Practice
SOP	Standard Operating Procedures
SOW	Statement of Work
SP	Surveillance Processing
SPAS	System Performance Analysis System
SPIFR	Single Pilot IFR
SRAP	Sensor Receiver and Processor
SRM	Safety Risk Management
SRM	Single Pilot Resource Management
SRMD	Safety Risk Management Document
SRMDM	Safety Risk Management Memo
SRS	Shuttle Reservation System
SRTM	Shuttle Radar Topography Mission
SSALF	SSALS with Sequenced Flashers
SSALR	Simplified Short Approach Lighting System
SSB	Single Side Band

SSC	System Support Center
SSC	Systems Support Center
SSD	System Support Directive
SSE	Servicing Security Element
SSM	System Support Modification
SSRWG	Systems Safety Risk Working Group
SST	System Shakedown Testing
ST&E	Security Test and Evaluation
STAMP	Site Transition Activation Management Plan
STAR	Standard Terminal Arrival Route
STAR	Standard Terminal Arrivals
STARS	Standard Terminal Automation Replacement System
STC	Supplemental Type Certificate
STD	Standard
STMP	Special Traffic Management Program
STMUX	Statistical Data Multiplexer
STOL	Short Take - Off and Landing
STOL	Short Takeoff and Landing
STR	System Technical Release
STT	Staffing to Traffic
STVS	Small Tower Voice Switch
SUA	Special Use Airspace
SUP	Suspected Unapproved Parts
SUPCOM	Supervisors Committee (AAT AND AAF)
SUPPS	Supplementary Procedures
SURPIC	Surface Picture
SVCA	Service A
SVCB	Service B
SVCC	Service C
SVCO	Service O
SVFB	Interphone Service F (B)
SVFC	Interphone Service F (C)
SVFD	Interphone Service F (D)
SVFO	Interphone Service F (A)
SVFR	Special Visual Flight Rules
SWAP	Severe Weather Avoidance Procedure/Program

SWIFT	Selections Within Faster Times
SWIM	System Wide Information Management
SWPPP	Storm Water Pollution Protection Plan
T1MUX	T1 Multiplexer
TAAS	Terminal Advance Automation System
TAC	Tactical Air Command (USAF) Tester
TAC	Terminal Area Chart
TACAN	Tactical Air Navigation
TACAN	Tactical Aircraft Control and Navigation
TACR	TACAN at VOR, TACAN only
TAF	Terminal Area Forecast
TAMR	Terminal Automation Modernization and Replacement
TARS	Terminal Automated Radar Service
TAS	True Air Speed
TATCA	Terminal Air Traffic Control Automation
TAVT	Terminal Airspace Visualization Tool
TAWS	Terrain Awareness and Warning System
TBFM	Time Based Flow Management
TBO	Trajectory Based Operation
TCA	Tactical Customer Advocate
TCA	Terminal Control Area
TCA	Traffic Control Airport or Tower Control Airport
TCACCIS	Transportation Coordinator Automated Command and Control Information System
TCAP	Traffic Count Automation Program
TCAS	Traffic Alert and Collision Avoidance System
TCC	DOT Transportation Computer Center
TCCC	Tower Control Computer Complex
TCE	Tone Control Equipment
TCLT	Tentative Calculated Landing Time
TCO	Telecommunications Certification Officer
TCOM	Terminal Communications
TCS	Tower Communications System
TCVR	Transceiver
TDDS	Terminal Data Display System
TDLS	Tower Data-Link Services
TDMUX	Time Division Data Multiplexer

TDWR	Terminal Doppler Weather Radar
TELCO	Telephone Company
TELMS	Telecommunications Management System
TERP	Terminal Instrument Procedure
TFAC	To Facility
TFDM	Tower Flight Data Manager
TFM	Traffic Flow Management
TFMS	Traffic Flow Management System
TFR	Temporary Flight Restriction
TH	Threshold
TIB	Technical Instruction Book
TIMS	Telecommunications Information Management System
TIPH	Taxi Into Position and Hold
TIPS	Terminal Information Processing System
TL	Taxilane
TM&O	Telecommunications Management and Operations
TMA	Traffic Management Advisor
TMC	Traffic Management Coordinator
TMC	Travel Management Center
TMC/MC	Traffic Management Coordinator/Military Coordinator
TMCC	Terminal Information Processing System
TMCC	Traffic Management Computer Complex
TMF	Traffic Management Facility
TMI	Traffic Management Initiative
TML	Television Microwave Link
TMLI	Television Microwave Link Indicator
TMLR	Television Microwave Link Repeater
TMLT	Television Microwave Link Terminal
TMP	Traffic Management Processor
TMS	Traffic Management System
TMSPS	Traffic Management Specialists
TMU	Traffic Management Unit
TNAV	Terminal Navigational Aids
TOCC	Technical Operations Control Center
TODA	Takeoff Distance Available
TOF	Time Of Flight

TOFMS	Time of Flight Mass Spectrometer
TOPS	Telecommunications Ordering and Pricing System (GSA software tool)
TORA	Take-off Run Available
TP	Telecommunication Processor
TP	Track Processing
TPP	Terminal Procedures Publication
TPR	Technical Performance Record
TR	Telecommunications Request
TRACAB	Terminal Radar Approach Control in Tower Cab
TRACON	Terminal Radar Approach Control
TRACON	Terminal Radar Approach Control Facility
TRAD	Terminal Radar Service
TRB	Transportation Research Board
TRD	Technical Reference Data
TRDR	Technical Reference Data Record
TRNG	Training
TS	Top Secret
TSA	Taxiway Safety Area
TSARTS	Terminal Stand-Alone Radar Training System
TSARTS	Terminal Stand-Alone Radar Training System
TSC	Technical Support Center
TSD	Traffic Situation Display
TSD	Traffic Situational Display
TSEC	Terminal Secondary Radar Service
TSO	Technical Standard Order
TSP	Telecommunications Service Priority
TSR	Telecommunications Service Request
TSS	Tower Simulation System
TSSC	Technical Support Services Contract
TSYS	Terminal Equipment Systems
TTMA	TRACON Traffic Management Advisor
TTWG	Technical Transfer Working Group
TTY	Teletype
TUR	Time Utilization Report
TVOR	Terminal VHF Omnidirectional Range
TVSR	Terminal Voice Switch Replacement

TW	Taxiway
TWEB	Transcribed Weather Broadcast
TWIP	Terminal Weather Information for Pilots
TWR	Tower (non-controlled)
TWY	Taxiway
TX	Transmitter
TY	Type (FAACIS)
UAS	Uniform Accounting System
UAS	Unmanned Aircraft Systems
UAT	Universal Access Transceiver
UBA	User Benefits Applications
UBI	User Benefits Infrastructure
UCR	Unsatisfactory Condition Report
UFAS	Uniform Federal Accessibility Standard
UHF	Ultra High Frequency
UNIX	Uniplexed Information and Computing System
UPR	User Preferred Route
UPS	Uninterruptable Power Supply
UPT	User Preferred Trajectory
URA	Uniform Relocation Assistance and Real Property Acquisition Policies Act of 1970
URET	User Request Evaluation Tool
USAF	United States Air Force
USC	United States Code
USCG	United States Coast Guard
USG	United States Government
USNS	United States Notices to Airmen System
USOAP	Universal Safety Oversight Audit Program
USOC	Uniform Service Order Code
UTC	Coordinated Universal Time (ZULU)
VALE	Voluntary Airport Low Emission
VALE	Voluntary Airport Low Emission Program
VASI	Visual Approach Slope Indicator
VBScript	Visual Basic Scripting Edition
VDF	Very High Frequency Direction-Finding Station
VDL	Very High Frequency Data Link
VDME	VOR with Distance Measuring Equipment

VEARS	VSCS Emergency Access Radio System
VF	Voice Frequency
VFR	Visual Flight Rules
VGSI	Visual Guidance Slope Indicator
VHF	Very High Frequency
VLF	Very Low Frequency
VLJ	Very Light Jet
VMC	Visual Meteorological Conditions
VMS	Virtual Memory System
VNAV	Visual Navigational Aids
VNTSC	Volpe National Transportation System Center
VOIP	Voice Over Internet Protocol
VON	Virtual On-net
VOR	Very High Frequency Omnidirectional Range
VOR/DME	Very High Frequency Omnidirectional Range Collocated with Distance Measuring Equipment
VOR/DME	VHF Omnidirectional Range/Distance Measuring Equipment
VORTAC	Very High Frequency Omnidirectional Range Collocated Tactical Air
VORTAC	VOR collocated with TACAN
VOT	VOR Test Facility
V/PD	Vehicle/Pedestrian Deviation
VRRP	Voice Recorder Replacement Program
VRS	Voice Recording System
VSBP	Voice Switch Bypass
VSCS	Voice Switching and Control System
VTA	Vertex Time of Arrival
VTAC	VOR collocated with TACAN
VTOL	Vertical Take-off and landing
VTS	Voice Telecommunications System
WAAS	Wide Area Augmentation System
WADGPS	Wide Area Differential Global Positioning System
WAN	Wide Area Network
WARP	Weather and Radar Processor
WASS	Wide Area Augmentation System - GPS
WBS	Work Breakdown Structure
WC	Work Center
WCAM	Weather Camera

WCIS	Workmen's Compensation Information System
WCP	Weather Communications Processor
WECO	Western Electric Company
WESCOM	Western Electric Satellite Communications
WFD	Widespread Fatigue Damage
WG	Working Group
WiFi	Wireless Fidelity
WJHTC	William J. Hughes Technical Center
WMS	Web Map Service
WMS	Wide-area Master Station
WMSC	Weather Message Switching Center
WMSCR	Weather Message Switching Center Replacement
WOCC	Washington Operations Center Complex
WRS	Wide Area Augmentation System Reference Station
WRS	Wide-area Reference Station
WSA	Western Service Area
WSC	Western Service Center
WSCMO	Weather Service Contract Meteorological Observatory
WSFO	Weather Service Forecast Office
WSO	Weather Service Office
WSP	Weather Systems Processor
WSR	Weather Surveillance Radar
WSUS	Windows Server Update Service
WTHR	Weather
WX	Weather
XML	eXtensible Markup Language
ZAB	Albuquerque ARTCC
ZAN	Anchorage ARTCC
ZAU	Chicago ARTCC
ZBW	Boston ARTCC
ZDC	Washington ARTCC
ZDV	Denver ARTCC
ZFW	Fort Worth ARTCC
ZHU	Houston ARTCC
ZID	Indianapolis ARTCC
ZJX	Jacksonville ARTCC

ZKC	Kansas City ARTCC
ZLA	Los Angeles ARTCC
ZLC	Salt Lake City ARTCC
ZMA	Miami ARTCC
ZME	Memphis ARTCC
ZMP	Minneapolis ARTCC
ZNY	New York ARTCC
ZOA	Oakland ARTCC
ZOB	Cleveland ARTCC
ZSE	Seattle ARTCC
ZTL	Atlanta ARTCC

Aviation Jargons

A Glossary of Aviation Acronyms [Aviation Terms and Definitions]

Aviation Jargon is sometimes a confusing and frustrating language and full three, four or more letter acronyms which can catch out even the knowledgeable! Sometime the picture is further confused by a single acronym having a number of meanings depending on the context in which it is used.

Take for example the acronym IFE, it has several meanings depending on the area of Aviation it relates to, it can mean 'In- Flight Emergency', 'In-Flight Entertainment' or 'International Flight Engineers'. Confused?

Hopefully you won't be with the Jargon Buster you may be able to successfully navigate the multitude of meanings.

The listing is in alphabetical order for easier navigation. We hope it helps.

Acronym Meaning

A-VDGS	Advanced-Visual Docking Guidance System
A/A	Air to air
A/G	Air/Ground
A&F	IFALPA Administration & Finance Committee
A&P	Airframe & Powerplant (US FAA)
AAA	Aesean Airline Association
AAC	Airline Administrative Communication
AACC	Airport Associations Co-coordinating Council
AACO	Arab Air Carriers Organization
AAIB	Air Accidents Investigation Branch (UK)
AALPBH	Association of Airline Pilots in Bosnia & Herzegovina
AAM	Airbus Asset Management

AAME	Association of Aviation Medical Examiners
AAPA	Association of Asia Pacific Airlines
AASA	Air Lines Association of Southern Africa
AATF	Airworthiness Assurance Task Force
ABET	Airspace Behavioral Engineering Technology
ABM	Abeam
ABV	Above
AC	Altocumulus
ACA	Austrian Cockpit Association
VDR VHF	(Very High Frequency) Digital Radio
VFOP	Visual Flight Rules Operations Panel
VFR	Visual Flight Rules
VFRG	Visual Flight Rules Group
VHF	Very High Frequency
VKB KLM	Flight Engineers Association
VLDM	Very low dispersible material
VMP	Vertical Measurement Panel
VNV	Vereniging van Nederlandse Verkeersvliegers (Dutch Air Line Pilots' Association)
VTOL	Vertical Take-Off & Landing
WAAS	Wide Area Augmentation System
WAFS	World Area Forecast System Study Group
WFTU	World Federation of Trade Unions
WG	Working Group
WGS 84	World Geodetic System 1984
WHO	World Health Organisation
WIAS	Weather Information Automated System
WIST	Study Group on Low Level Wind Shear Turbulence (ICAO)
WMO	World Meteorological Organisation
WOCL	Window of Circadian Low
WP	Work Package
WXXM	Weather eXchange Model
XPDR	Transponder
YOYO	Only Y Available
Zulu or	Equivalent to Greenwich Mean Time or UTC

FAQ

1. What is the Minimum Eligibility for taking Pilot Training course?

The minimum requirement to get enrolled for Pilot Training course in India/Nepal is 12th pass from a recognized board & above (PCM) and 17years. Rest most of the countries is minimum 10 Years of Schooling only.

2. What is the total Investment [Fees] amount for the entire course?

The actual Pilot Training starts after a student has successfully appeared in a Pre Flight Training that is for 1-2 weeks in India & Flight Training in Canada, Philippines, New Zealand, Sri Lanka, U.S.A. The cost of Pre Flight Training is Rs.25,000. and Flight Training cost is different for different countries and schools like in New Zealand it is NZ $ 65000- $ 90,000, in Philippines - USD $ 40500 – USD $ 60,000, in USA - $ 45000 – USD $ 1,00,000, in Canada - CAD $ 55000 – CAD $ 85,000 and in Sri Lanka - US$ 45000 – USD $ 75,000. In India Pilot Training may be little cheap between INR Rs 20,000,00 to Rs 35,000,00 but quality of Flying Training also may not be as good as you get Internationally.

3. What are the different Pilot's Licenses available?

PPL - Private Pilot License

CPL - Commercial Pilot License

ATPL - Airline Transport Pilot License

CFI - Chief Flight Instructor

4. What is the Salary of an Airline Pilot?

The salary is one difficult subject to generalize on as salaries vary extensively around the world. Crop spraying is renowned as being a very well paid Pilot's Job but this will be cyclically dependant on the seasons. Internationally, Salary of the Second Officer ranges between USD $ 600 per month to USD $ 1500 per month; First Officer USD $ 1000 per month to USD $ 3500 per month and for a Captain between USD $ 2000 per month to USD $ 8500 per month. The salary depends on the Airline you fly and the number of hours/years of service.

Normally the period of transition from a First Officer to a Captain is 5-15 years. Few fortunate Pilots become a Captain in 2-5 years too. Similarly, Pilot salaries have drasticaslly fallen down after the shut down of so many small and medium Airlineses due to Global Aviation Recession.

5. What are the job prospects?

Due to Global Reccession, Aviation Industry is going through a rough phase. But, with the economy growing consistently and increasing purchasing power of people across the globle the industry is bound to grow. The importance of time over money is key to making a transition from the railways to Airlines as a primary mode of transport. Flying however is a universal skill and once you have a few thousand hours under the belt, the world is open with opportunities.

6. What are the Job opportunity after the completion of course?

With the prevailing recession and damping condition of industry, Job opportunity do exist but only few for now. and so if you are are a quality Pilot with passion and sincerity then it is not difficult to get placed in good Airlines. Also, with growing Business Aviation across the industry Pilots would obviously be required. Moreover, We train you to grab those opportunities by our best CV data bank. Here all you need is to submit your CV in a prescribed format and send it to us on bestcvdatabank@ gmail.com and we help you to get in touch with best employers.

7. Which are the subjects that need to be studied along with Flying hours?

Air Navigation, Meteorology, Air Regulation, Aircraft and instruments in general and specific and Radio Aids and Instruments

8. Is any conversion required to fly in other countries?

Yes, conversion is required to fly in different countries and each place has different rules.

List of Aircrafts

Aérospatiale AS-350 Écureuil & AS-355 Écureuil 2 Light utility helicopters

Aérospatiale SA-360/361/365C Dauphin Mid size utility helicopters

Aérospatiale SN-601 Corvette Light corporate Jet

Aérospatiale-British Aerospace Concorde Medium Range supersonic Airliner

Aerokopter AK1-3 "Sanka" Light two seats helicopter

Agusta A109 Twin engined utility & corporate helicopter

Agusta A119 Koala Light utility helicopter

Ahrens AR 404 four engine Turboprop utility Aircraft

Air Tractor series of piston & Turboprop powered agricultural Aircraft

Airbus A300B2/B4 Medium Range Widebody Airliner

Airbus A300-600 Medium Range Widebody Airliner

Airbus Beluga very large cargo Aircraft

Airbus A310-200 Medium to long Range Widebody Airliner

Airbus A310-300 Medium to long Range Widebody Airliner

Airbus A318 100 seat regional Airliner

Airbus A319 Medium Range Airliner

Airbus A319CJ Long Range large corporate Jet

Airbus A320 Short to medium Range Airliner

Airbus A321 Short to medium Range narrowbody Airliner

Airbus A330-200 Medium to long Range Widebody Airliner

Airbus A330-300 Large capacity medium to long Range Airliner

Airbus A340-200 Long Range Widebody Airliner

Airbus A340-300 Long Range Widebody Airliner

Airbus A340-500 Ultra long Range Widebody Airliner

Airbus A340-600 Long Range Widebody Airliner

Airbus A350-800 Long Range Widebody Airliner

Airbus A350-900 Long Range Widebody Airliner

Airbus A350-1000 Long Range Widebody Airliner

Airbus A380 Long Range high capacity Widebody Airliner

Alpha 2000 The Robin R2000 now manufactured in New Zealand

American Aviation AA-1 Yankee two seat Light Aircraft

American Aviation AA-1A Trainer two seat Light training Aircraft

American Aviation AA-2 Patriot four seat Light Aircraft prototype

American Champion & Bellanca series Series of two seat utility and aerobatic Light Aircraft

Antonov/PZL Mielec An-2 Bi Plane utility Transport

Antonov An-10 110 Passenger Turboprop

Antonov An-12 Turboprop cargo Aircraft

Antonov An-22 Antheus Large capacity Turboprop cargo Aircraft

Antonov An-24 44-50 Passenger Airliner and utility Aircraft

Antonov/PZL Mielec An-28 Regional Airliner and utility Transport

Antonov An-30 aerial survey Aircraft

Antonov An-38 Regional Airliner and utility Transport

Antonov An-70 Heavylift propfan cargo Aircraft

Antonov An-72 & An-74 STOL capable utility Transport

Antonov An-124 Ruslan Heavylift freighter

Antonov An-140 50 Passenger short-Range Turboprop Airliner

Antonov An-225 Mriya Extra-Large cargo Aircraft

APM 20 Lionceau Very Light utility Aircraft

APM 30 Lion Light utility Aircraft

Arado S I & S III two seat trainers

Arado SC I two seat trainer

Arado SC II two seat trainer

Arado L I two seat Light Aircraft

Arado L II two seat Light Aircraft

Arado V I prototype four Passenger Airliner and Air mail carrier

Arado W 2 two seat sea Plane trainer

Armstrong Whitworth Ape experimental Aircraft

Armstrong Whitworth Argosy three engine Bi Plane Airliner

Armstrong Whitworth Atalanta nine Passenger four engine Airliner

Armstrong Whitworth Ensign 40 Passenger four engine Airliner

Armstrong Whitworth A.W.52 flying wing experimental Aircraft

Armstrong Whitworth Argosy four engine Turboprop cargo Aircraft

Arrow Sport two seat Light Aircraft

Arrow Model F two seat Light Aircraft

ATR ATR-42 42 seat Turboprop regional Airliner

ATR ATR-72 70 seat Turboprop regional Airliner

Auster J-1 Autocrat three seat Light Aircraft

Auster J-1U Workmaster agricultural Aircraft

Auster J-2 Arrow two seat Light Aircraft

Auster J-3 Atom two seat Light Aircraft

Auster J-4 two seat Light Aircraft

Auster Avis prototype Light utility Aircraft

Auster Autocar four seat Light Aircraft

Auster Aiglet Trainer aerobatic four seat Light Aircraft

Auster Alpine four seat Light Aircraft

Auster B.4 prototype Light cargo Aircraft

Auster Agricola agricultural Aircraft

Auster D.4 two seat Light Aircraft

Avia BH-1 two seat Light Aircraft

Avia BH-5 two seat Light Aircraft

Avia BH-9 two seat Light Aircraft

Avia BH-10 single seat aerobatic Aircraft

Avia BH-12 two seat Light Aircraft

Avia BH-16 single seat Light Aircraft

Avia BH-20 two seat trainer

Avia BH-25 Bi Plane Airliner

Avia 14 28 Passenger Airliner

Aviat Husky Two seat utility Light Aircraft

Aviat Pitts Special Single and two seat competition aerobatic Bi Planes

Aviation Traders ATL-90 Accountant prototype 28 Passenger Turboprop Airliner

Aviation Traders ATL-98 CarvAir Freighter/utility Transport

Avro Baby single seat Light Aircraft

Avro Avian two seat Light Aircraft

Avro 618 Ten ten Passenger Airliner

Avro 652 four Passenger Airliner

Avro York four engine Airliner & cargo Aircraft

Avro Tudor four engine Airliner

Avro 748 (a.k.a. HS 748 & BAe 748) 50 seat Turboprop Airliner

Avro RJ Series See British Aerospace BAe 146

Avro Canada Jetliner prototype Jet Airliner

Ayres Let L 610 40 seat regional Airliner

Ayres Thrush & Rockwell Thrush Commander Agricultural Aircraft

B

BAC One-Eleven Short haul Airliner

Baade B-152 also known as Dresden 152 was the first German Passenger Jet Airliner

Beagle Airedale Four seat Light Aircraft

Beagle D5 Husky Light Aircraft

Beagle Pup Two, three and four place Light Aircraft

Beagle Terrier three seat Light Aircraft

Beagle B.206 Six/eight place cabin twin

Bede BD-1 two place prototype design

Bede BD-5 single seat sport Aircraft

Beechcraft Model 17 Staggerwing high performance Light Aircraft

Beechcraft Model 18 Twin Beech Light utility Transport

Beechcraft Model 19 Musketeer Four seat Light Aircraft

Beechcraft Model 23 Sundowner Four seat Light Aircraft

Beechcraft Model 24 Sierra Four seat Light Aircraft

Beechcraft Model 33, 35 & 36 Bonanza Four & six seat high performance Light Aircraft

Beechcraft Model 50 Twin Bonanza Six place Light Business twin

Beechcraft Model 55, 56 & 58 Baron Four or six place Light Business twin

Beechcraft Model 60 Duke Four or six place high performance twin

Beechcraft Model 65, 70, 80, 85 & 88 Queen Air Utility, Light executive Transport, commuter Airliner, Air Ambulance

Beechcraft Model 76 Duchess Four place Light twin

Beechcraft Model 77 Skipper Two seat pilot training Aircraft

Beechcraft Model 90 King Air 6-10 seat Executive Transport, Commuter Airliner, Air Ambulance, Freight Transport

Beechcraft Model 95 Travel Air Four place Light twin

Beechcraft Model 99 Airliner 19 seat Commuter Airliner

Beechcraft Model 100 King Air 8-12 seat Executive Transport, Commuter Airliner, Air Ambulance, Freight Transport

Beechcraft Model 200 (Super) King Air 8-12 seat Executive Transport, Commuter Airliner, Air Ambulance, Freight Transport, Aerial Survey Aircraft

Beechcraft Model 300 (Super) King Air 8-14 seat Executive Transport, Commuter Airliner, Air Ambulance, Freight Transport, Aerial Survey Aircraft

Beechcraft Model 1300 Airliner 13 seat Commuter Airliner

Beechcraft Model 1900 Airliner 19 seat Regional Airliner and Corporate Transport

Beechcraft Model 400 BeechJet Light corporate Jet

Beechcraft Starship 2000 Advanced technology corporate Transport

Bell 47 Two or three seat Light utility helicopter

Bell 204 & 205 Medium Lift Utility helicopter

Bell 206 JetRanger Light utility helicopter

Bell 206L LongRanger Light utility helicopter

Bell 212 Twin TwoTwelve Medium lift utility helicopter

Bell 214B and 214ST Medium Transport helicopter

Bell 222 & 230 Twin engine Light utility helicopters

Bell 407 Seven place utility helicopter

Bell 412 Medium lift utility helicopter

Bell 427 Light twin utility helicopters

Bell 429 Light/intermediate twin utility helicopters

Bell 430 Twin engine intermediate size helicopter

Bell BA 609 Six to nine seat corporate/ utility tiltrotor

Bell 206LT TwinRanger & TridAir Gemini ST Twin engine Light utility helicopters

Beriev Be-30/Be-32 Regional Airliner and utility Transport

Beriev Be-103 Firefighting and Multirole Maritime Amphibian

Beriev Be-112 Firefighting and Multirole Maritime Amphibian

Beriev Be-200 Firefighting and multirole amphibian

Beriev Be-2500 Proposed amphibian freighter

Boeing Model 40 Bi Plane Air mail carrier/Airliner

Boeing Model 80 Bi Plane Airliner

Boeing Model 221 Air mail carrier

Boeing 247 propeller Airliner

Boeing 307 Stratoliner propeller Airliner

Boeing 314 Clipper FLying boat Airliner

Boeing 367-80 Jet Transport development Aircraft

Boeing 377 Stratocruiser propeller Airliner

Boeing 707-100 Medium to long Range Airliner and freighter

Boeing 717 Short to medium Range Airliner

Boeing 720 Medium Range narrowbody Airliner

Boeing 727-100 Short to medium Range narrowbody Airliner

Boeing 727-200 Short to medium Range narrowbody Airliner

Boeing 737-100/200 Short Range narrowbody Airliner

Boeing 737-300/400/500 Short to medium Range narrowbody Airliner

Boeing 737-600/700 Short to medium Range Airliners

Boeing 737-800/900 Short to medium Range Airliners

Boeing 747-100 Long Range high capacity Widebody Airliner

Boeing 747-200 Long Range high capacity Widebody Airliner

Boeing 747-300 Long Range high capacity Widebody Airliner

Boeing 747-400 Long Range high capacity Widebody Airliner

Boeing 747-8 Long Range high capacity Widebody Airliner

Boeing 747SP Long Range high capacity Widebody Airliner

Boeing 757-200 Medium Range narrowbody Airliner

Boeing 757-300 Medium Range narrowbody Airliner

Boeing 767-200 Medium to long Range Widebody Airliner

Boeing 767-300 Medium to long Range Widebody Airliner

Boeing 767-400 Medium to long Range Widebody Airliner

Boeing 777-200 Long and ultra long Range Widebody Airliners

Boeing 777-300 Long Range high capacity Widebody Airliner

Boeing 787-3 Medium Range high capacity Widebody Airliner

Boeing 787-8 Long to Ultra-Long Range high capacity Widebody Airliner

Boeing 787-9 Long to Ultra-Long Range high capacity Widebody Airliner

Boeing Business Jet Long Range large capacity corporate Jet

Boeing 2707 Supersonic Transport project

Boeing Vertol (Kawasaki) KV 107 Medium to heavylift utility helicopter

Boeing Commercial Chinook Heavylift utility and Airliner helicopter

Boeing/MDHS/Hughes 500 Light utility helicopters

Boeing MD 520N Light utility helicopter

Boeing MD 600N Eight place Light utility helicopter

Boeing MD Explorer Light twin helicopter

Boeing Stearman Two seat sport, utility and agricultural Bi Plane

Bombardier BD-100 Challenger 300 Super mid size corporate Jet

Bombardier CL600 Challenger 600/601/604/605 long Range corporate Jets

Bombardier Challenger 850 large long Range corporate Jet

Bombardier Global 5000 long Range high capacity corporate Jet

Bombardier BD-700 Global Express Ultra long Range, high speed, high capacity corporate Jet

Bombardier LearJet 40 small corporate Jet

Bombardier LearJet 45 Mid-size corporate Jet

Bombardier LearJet 55 & 60 Mid-size corporate Jets

Brantly B-2 & 305 Light piston powered utility helicopters

Bristol 167 Brabazon long Range Airliner

Bristol 170 Freighter Short Range freighter/utility Transport

Bristol 175 Britannia long Range Turboprop Airliner

British Aerospace Jetstream 31 18 seat regional Turboprop Airliner

British Aerospace Jetstream 41 29 seat regional Turboprop Airliner

British Aerospace/Hawker Siddeley 748 Turboprop Regional Airliner

British Aerospace ATP Turboprop powered regional Airliner

British Aerospace BAe 125 Mid-size corporate Jet

British Aerospace BAe 146 four engined regional Jet Airliner

Britten-Norman BN-2 Islander Commuter Airliner and Light utility Transport

Britten-Norman BN-2A Mk III Trislander Commuter Airliner

C

CanadAir CL-215 & CanadAir CL-415 Firebomber and utility amphibian

CanadAir CL-44 & Yukon Medium to long Range Airliner and freighter

CanadAir CL-600 Challenger 600 Medium to long Range Widebody corporate Jet

CanadAir CL-600 Challenger 601 & 604 Long Range Widebody corporate Jets

CanadAir CL-600 Regional Jet CRJ-100 & 200 Regional Jet Airliner

CanadAir CL-600 Regional Jet CRJ-700 70 seat regional Jet Airliner

CAP Aviation CAP-10/20/21/230/231/232 Single and two seat aerobatic Light Aircraft

CASA C212 Aviocar STOL Turboprop regional Airliner and utility Transport

CASA/IPTN CN235 Utility Transport and 45 seat regional Airliner

Cessna 120

Cessna 140

Cessna 150 & Cessna 152 Two seat primary and aerobatic capable trainers

Cessna 170 Four seat Light Aircraft

Cessna 172 Skyhawk

Cessna 175 Skylark Four seat Light Aircraft

Cessna 177 Cardinal and Cardinal RG Four seat Light Aircraft

Cessna 180 & 185 Skywagon Four to six seat utility Light Aircraft

Cessna 182 High performance four seat Light Aircraft

Cessna 188 AGwagon, AGpickup, AGtruck, and AGhusky series of agricultural Aircraft

Cessna 205, 206 & 207 Six seat utility Light Aircraft

Cessna 208 Caravan I, Grand Caravan & Cargomaster Single Turboprop utility Transport

Cessna 210 Centurion High performance four to six seat Light Aircraft

Cessna 310 & 320 Skynight Four to six seat Light piston twins

Cessna 336 & 337 Skymaster Six seat Light piston twins

Cessna 340 & 335 Six seat Business twins

Cessna 404 Titan Ten place corporate, commuter and freighter Transport

Cessna 411, 401 & 402 Freighter, 10 seat commuter, or six to eight seat Business twins

Cessna 421 & 414 Pressurised six to eight seat cabin twins

Cessna 500 & 501 Citation, Citation I & Citation I/SP Light corporate Jets

Cessna 550 Citation II & 551 Citation II & Bravo Light corporate Jets

Cessna 560 Citation V, Ultra & Ultra Encore Small to midsize corporate Jet

Cessna 560XL Citation Excel Small to mid size corporate Jet

Cessna 650 Citation III, VI & VII Medium size corporate Jets

Cessna 680 Citation Sovereign Mid size corporate Jet

Cessna Citation X Long Range, high speed, mid size corporate Jet

Cessna CitationJet, CJ1 & CJ2 Light corporate Jets

Cessna CorsAir, Caravan II Turboprop powered executive Transports

Cessna Conquest, Conquest I & II Turboprop powered executive Transports

Cessna T303 Crusader Six seat corporate and utility Transport

Chichester-Miles Leopard High performance Jet powered four seat Light Aircraft

Cirrus SR20/22 Four seat high performance Light Aircraft

Citabria series of tandem 2 seat high wing, aerobatic, utility and STOL Aircraft

Christen Eagle, aerobatic kit Aircraft, based on Pitts Special

Columbia 400 Four seat high performance Light Aircraft

Commander 114B Four seat high performance Light Aircraft

Concorde

Conroy CL-44-0 Skymonster Large freighter

ConvAir 240/340/440 Short haul commercial Transports

ConvAir CV-540/580/600/640/5800 Short haul Turboprop converted commercial ransports

Curtiss C46 Commando Freighter

D

Dassault Falcon 2000 Transcontinental Range mid to large size corporate Jet

Dassault Falcon 50 Long Range mid size corporate Jet

Dassault Falcon 900 Large transcontinental Range corporate Jet

Dassault Falcon 7X Large transcontinental Range corporate Jet

Dassault Mercure Short to medium Range narrowbody Jet

Dassault Mystère/Falcon 10 & 100 Light corporate Jet

Dassault Mystère/Falcon 20 & 200 Mid size corporate Jet and multirole utility Transport

De Havilland Canada DHC-1 Chipmunk Two seat Light Aircraft

De Havilland Canada DHC-2 Beaver STOL utility Transport

De Havilland Canada DHC-3 Otter STOL utility Transport

De Havilland Canada DHC-4 Caribou STOL utility Transport

De Havilland Canada DHC-5 Buffalo STOL utility Transport

De Havilland Canada DHC-6 Twin Otter STOL Turboprop regional Airliner and utility Transport

De Havilland Canada Dash 7 STOL Four Turboprop regional Airliner

De Havilland Canada DHC-8-100/200 Dash 8 Twin Turboprop regional Airliner

De Havilland Canada DHC-8-300 Dash 8 Twin Turboprop regional Airliner

De Havilland Canada DHC-8-400 Dash 8 70 seat Twin Turboprop regional Airliner

De Havilland Comet the world's first commercial Jet Airliner

De Havilland DH.86 1930's Bi Plane Airliner

De Havilland DH.89 Dragon Rapide 1930's Bi Plane Airliner

De Havilland DH.104 Dove Eight seat commuter Airliner and executive Transport

De Havilland DH.114 Heron 14 seat commuter Airliner

De Havilland DH.82 Tiger Moth Two seat Bi Plane Light Aircraft

Diamond DA20 Two seat Light Aircraft and basic trainer

Dornier Do 27 Four to six seat STOL utility Light Aircraft

Dornier Do 28 & 128 STOL utility Transports

Dornier Do 228 Turboprop utility Aircraft

Dornier Do 328 Turboprop and turboJet Aircraft

Douglas DC-3 Short Range Airliner and utility Transport

Douglas DC-4 Piston engined Airliner and freighter

Douglas DC-6 Piston engined Airliner and freighter

Douglas DC-7 Piston engine Airliner and freighter

Douglas DC-8 Series 10 to 50 Medium to long Range Airliner and freighter

Douglas DC-8 Super 60 & 70 Series Long Range medium capacity Airliner and freighter

E

Edgley Optica British Light Aircraft

EH Industries EH 101 Commuter, offshore oil rig support & utility helicopter

Embraer EMB 110 Bandeirante 15-18 seat Turboprop multi-purpose Aircraft

Embraer EMB 120 Brasilia 30 seat Turboprop regional Airliner

Embraer EMB 121 Xingu 8-9 seat Turboprop multi-purpose Aircraft

Embraer/FMA CBA 123 Vector 19 seat Turboprop regional Airliner

Embraer ERJ 135 37 seat regional Jet Airliner

Embraer ERJ 140 45 seat regional Jet Airliner

Embraer ERJ 145 50 seat regional Jet Airliner

Embraer 170 70 seat medium Range Jet Airliner

Embraer 175 78 seat medium Range Jet Airliner

Embraer 190 98 seat medium Range Jet Airliner

Embraer 195 108 seat medium Range Jet Airliner

Embraer Lineage 1000 corporate Jet based on the Embraer 190 platform

Embraer Legacy 600 corporate Jet based on the Embraer ERJ 145 platform

Embraer Phenom 100 very Light corporate Jet

Embraer Phenom 300 Light corporate Jet

Enstrom F-28/280/480 Three and five seat Light helicopters

ERCO Ercoupe and derivatives Two-seat Light Aircraft

Eurocopter Super Puma Medium lift utility helicopter

Eurocopter Ecureuil Light utility helicopter

Eurocopter AS-355 Ecureuil 2 Twin engined Light utility helicopter

Eurocopter AS-365N Dauphin 2 & EC-155 Twin engine mid sized utility helicopter

Eurocopter BO 105 & EC Super Five Five place multi purpose Light utility helicopter

Eurocopter Colibri Five place Light utility helicopter

Eurocopter EC-135/635 Seven place Light twin turbine utility helicopter

MBB/Kawasaki BK117 Twin engine utility helicopter

Exec 162F Two-seat kit helicopter, manufactured by RotorWay International

Extra 230, 300 & 200 Unlimited competition aerobatic Aircraft

F

FAirchild (Swearingen) Merlin Turboprop corporate Transport

FAirchild Aerospace 228 15-19 seat regional Airliner and STOL utility Transport

FAirchild Aerospace 328 30 seat regional Turboprop Airliner

FAirchild Aerospace 328Jet & 428Jet 32 seat regional Jet Airliner

FAirchild Aerospace Metro II, III & 23 19 seat regional Airliner

FFA AS-202 Bravo Two seat basic trainer and aerobatic Light Aircraft

Fokker 50 Turboprop regional Airliner

Fokker 70 70 seat regional Jetliner

Fokker F100 100 seat regional Jet

Fokker F27 & FAirchild F-27 & FH-227 Regional Airliners

Fokker F-28 Fellowship Regional Jet Airliner

Fokker F-VII

Ford Trimotor

Fuji FA200 Aero Subaru Four seat Light Aircraft

G

GAF N22 & N24 Nomad STOL utility Transport

Gippsland GA200 "Fatman" Two seat agricultural Aircraft

Gippsland GA8 "Airvan" Eight seat utility Light Aircraft

Grob G 115 Two seat basic and aerobatic trainer

Grob GF 200 Four seat high performance Light Aircraft

Grumman American AA-1B Trainer Two seat Light Aircraft

Grumman American AA-5 Traveler, Tiger & Cheetah Four seat Light Aircraft

Grumman G-1159 Gulfstream II/III Long Range large corporate Jet

Grumman G-159 Gulfstream I Corporate Transport and regional Airliner

Grumman G-164 Ag-Cat Bi Plane agricultural Aircraft

Grumman G-21 "Goose" Eight seat utility amphibian

Grumman G-44 "Widgeon" Light utility amphibian

Grumman G-73 "Mallard" Ten seat utility amphibious Transport

Grumman HU-16 "Albatross" Amphibious Airliner and Light utility Transport

Gulfstream American GA-7 Cougar four place Light twin-engined Aircraft

Gulfstream Aerospace Gulfstream IV G-IV Long Range large corporate Transport

Gulfstream Aerospace Gulfstream V G-V Ultra long Range large corporate Transport

Gulfstream Aerospace Jetprop & Turbo Commander Twin Turboprop utility and corporate Transports

H

Handley Page Herald Turboprop Airliner and freighter

Handley Page Jetstream 12 seat regional Turboprop Airliner

Harbin Y-11/12 Commuter Airliners and utility Transports

Hawker Siddeley H.S.125-1/2/3/400/600 Mid-size corporate Jet

Hawker Siddeley HS 748 (a.k.a. Avro 748)

Hawker Siddeley Trident-1/1E/2C/3B Short/Medium Range Airliner.

Helio Courier Four/six place STOL utility Light Aircraft

Hiller UH-12 Light utility helicopter

Hindustan Advanced Light Helicopter Medium utility helicopter

Honda HA-420 HondaJet Light corporate Jet

I

IAI Arava STOL utility Transport

IAI Westwind Small to mid size corporate Jet

Ilyushin Il-14 Short Range Airliner and utility Transport

Ilyushin Il-18 Medium Range Turboprop Airliner

Ilyushin Il-62 Medium to long Range medium capacity Airliner

Ilyushin Il-76 Medium to long Range Passenger

Ilyushin Il-76TF Medium to long Range freighter

Ilyushin Il-76MD

Ilyushin Il-76MF

Ilyushin Il-76MK

Ilyushin Il-76TF

Ilyushin Il-86 Medium Range Widebody Airliner

Ilyushin Il-96 Long Range Widebody Airliner

Ilyushin Il-96-300 Medium Range Widebody Airliner

Ilyushin Il-96-400 Medium Range Widebody Airliner

Ilyushin Il-96T Medium to long Range freighter

Ilyushin Il-96-400T Medium to long Range freighter

Ilyushin Il-112B

Ilyushin Il-103 Two and five seat Light Aircraft

Ilyushin Il-114 Turboprop regional Airliner

Ilyushin Il-114-100 Medium to long Range Passenger

Ilyushin MC-21

Ilyushin Il-MTC

IPTN N-250 64/68 seat Turboprop regional Airliner

Israel IAI-1125 Astra/Gulfstream G100 Small to mid size corporate Jet

Israel IAI-1126 Galaxy/Gulfstream G200 Super mid size corporate Transport

J

Junkers Ju 52

K

Kamov Ka-226 Medium size utility helicopter

Kaman K-1200 K-Max Aerial crane and utility helicopter

Kamov Ka-26 & Ka-226 Light twin engine utility and training helicopter

Kamov Ka-32 Medium size utility helicopter

Kamov Ka-50 Attack helicopter

Kamov Ka-52 Attack helicopter

Kestrel K250 Four to six place Light Aircraft

L

Lake LA4, Buccaneer & Renegade Four/six place amphibious Light Aircraft

LancAir LC-40 Columbia 300/350/400 High performance four seat Light Aircraft

Lear Jet 23, 24, 25, 28 & 29 Light corporate Jets

LearJet 35, 36 and LearJet 31 Light corporate Jets

Let L-40 MetaSokol Three/four seat Light Aircraft

Let L-410 & L-420 19 seat Turboprop regional Airliners

Let L-610 40 seat Turboprop regional Airliners

Let L-200 Morava Four/five seat Light twin

Lockheed C-130 Hercules Medium Range freighter

Lockheed JetStar Large size corporate Jet

Lockheed L-100 Hercules Medium Range freighter

Lockheed Constellation Long Range piston engine Airliner

Lockheed L-1011 TriStar 1/50/100/150/200/250 Medium to long Range Widebody Airliner

Lockheed L-1011 TriStar 500 Long Range Widebody Airliner

Lockheed L-188 Electra Turboprop Airliner and freighter

Luscombe Model 8 SilvAire Two seat Light Aircraft

Luscombe Spartan Four seat Light Aircraft

M

MA60 Turboprop regional Aircraft, from China

Martin 2-0-2 35- to 43-seat twin piston engined regional Airliner

Martin 4-0-4 40-seat twin piston engined regional Airliner

Maule M-4 to M-7 4-5 seat STOL capable Light Aircraft

McDonnell Douglas DC-10 & Boeing MD-10 Medium to long Range Widebody Airliner

McDonnell Douglas DC-9-10/20/30 Short Range Airliners

McDonnell Douglas DC-9-40/50 Short to medium Range Airliners

McDonnell Douglas MD-11 Long Range Widebody Airliner

McDonnell Douglas MD-81/82/83/88 Short to medium Range Airliner

McDonnell Douglas MD-87 Short to medium Range Airliner

McDonnell Douglas MD-90 Short to medium Range Airliner

MDM-1 Fox Two-seat aerobatic glider

Mil Mi-8/17 Medium lift utility helicopters

Mil Mi-26 Ultra heavy lift utility helicopter

Mil Mi-34 Two/four place Light helicopter

Millicer M10 AirTourer Two seat aerobatic capable Light Aircraft

Mitsubishi MU-2 Twin Turboprop utility Transport

Mooney M-20 to M-20G Four seat high performance Light Aircraft

Mooney M-20J to M-20S High performance four seat Light Aircraft

Mudry CAP10B (aka CAP-10) Two-seat side-by-side aerobatic trainer/competitor

N

NAL Saras Regional Turboprop Airliner (India) built by Hindustan aeronautics and NAL

NAMC YS-11 Twin Turboprop regional Airliner

Noorduyn Norseman 10 place utility Transport

North American Rockwell 100 Darter/Lark Commander Four seat Light Aircraft

North American/Ryan Navion High performance four/five seat Light Aircraft

O

Omega AircraftNew all metal MicroLight LSA VLA Two Seater Low wing

P

Pacific Aerospace CT-4 Airtrainer Two/three seat basic trainer

Pacific Aerospace Fletcher FU-24 Agricultural Aircraft

Pacific Aerospace Cresco Agricultural & Utility Aircraft

Pacific Aerospace 750XL Utility Aircraft

Partenavia P.68 Six/seven place Light twin

Piaggio P-166 Commuter Airliner and utility Transport

Piaggio P.180 Avanti Twin Turboprop executive Transport

Pilatus PC-12 Utility, regional Airliner and corporate Turboprop

Pilatus PC-6 Porter & Turbo Porter STOL utility Transport

Piper Aerostar Six seat high performance Light twin

Piper Cub Two seat Light Aircraft

Piper PA-18 Super Cub Two seat utility Light Aircraft

Piper PA-20 Pacer & PA-22 Tri-Pacer, Caribbean & Colt Two and four seat Light Aircraft

Piper PA-23 Apache & Aztec Four seat Light twins

Piper PA-24 Comanche Four seat high performance Light Aircraft

Piper PA-25 Pawnee Agricultural Aircraft

Piper PA-28 Cherokee Series Two and four seat Light Aircraft

Piper PA-28R Cherokee Arrow Four seat Light Aircraft

Piper PA-30/39 Twin Comanche Six seat Light twin

Piper PA-31 Chieftain/Mojave/T-1020/T-1040 Eight/ten seat corporate Transport and commuter Airliner

Piper PA-31 Navajo/Pressurized Navajo Six/eight seat corporate Transport and commuter Airliner

Piper PA-31T Cheyenne Twin Turboprop corporate Transports

Piper PA-32 Cherokee Six, Lance & Saratoga. Six seat high performance Light Aircraft

Piper PA-34 Seneca Six place Light twin

Piper PA-36 Pawnee Brave Agricultural Aircraft

Piper PA-38 Tomahawk Two seat Light Aircraft and basic trainer

Piper PA-42 Cheyenne III, IIIA & 400LS Twin Turboprop corporate Transports

Piper PA-44 Seminole Four seat Light twin

Piper PA-46 Malibu & Malibu Mirage. Six seat high performance Light Aircraft

Piper PA-46 Malibu Meridian Six seat corporate Turboprop

PZL-Mielec M-18 Dromader Ag spraying and firefighter Aircraft

PZL Mielec M-20 Mewa License-built Piper PA-34 Seneca

PZL Mielec M-28 Skytruck Light utility Aircraft

PZL Swidnik (Mil) Mi-2 Light twin turboshaft utility helicopter

PZL Swidnik Kania Light twin turboshaft utility helicopter

PZL Swidnik W-3 Sokól Mid size twin engine utility helicopter

PZL Swidnik SW-4 Puszczyk Light utility helicopter

PZL Warszawa-Okecie PZL-104 Wilga Four seat Light utility Aircraft

PZL Warszawa-Okecie PZL-110/111 Koliber Four seat Light Aircraft

R

Raytheon 390 Premier I Light corporate Jet

Beechcraft 1900 Regional Airliner and corporate Transport

Raytheon Beechcraft Baron Four or six place Business, utility & advanced pilot training twin

Raytheon Beechcraft Bonanza Four to six seat high performance Light Aircraft

Raytheon Beechcraft King Air 200 Twin Turboprop corporate, Passenger & utility Transport

Raytheon Beechcraft King Air 300 & 350 Turboprop powered corporate and utility Aircraft

Raytheon Beechcraft King Air 90 & 100 Twin Turboprop corporate and utility Transport

Raytheon Hawker 400XP (formerly BeechJet 400) Light corporate Jet

Raytheon Hawker 800 (formerly BAe 125) Mid-size corporate Jet

Raytheon Hawker 1000 Mid-size corporate Jet

Raytheon Hawker 4000 Super mid-size corporate Jet

Rearwin Ken-Royce A bi- Plane built in 1929 by Rearwin Air Planes

Rearwin Junior Small high wing mono Plane

Rearwin Speedster A narrow, streamlined Air Plane powered by Cirrus 90 or Menasco 125 HP

Rearwin Cloudster A popular enclosed cabin mono Plane

Rearwin Sportster Another popular Rearwin design from the early 1940s

Rearwin SkyRanger A small high-wing Air Plane somewhat similar to a Cessna

Republic RC-3 Seabee Four seat amphibious Light Aircraft

Robin DR400 & DR500 Four/five seat Light Aircraft

Robin R2000 & Robin HR200 Two seat training and aerobatic Light Aircraft

Robin R3000 Two/four seat Light Aircraft

Robin Aiglon Four seat Light Aircraft

Robinson R44 Four place piston engined Light helicopter

Robinson R22 Two seat piston engined Light helicopter

Rockwell 500/520/560/680/685/720 Commander Utility and corporate Transports

Rockwell Commander 112 & 114 Four seat high performance Light Aircraft

Rockwell Sabreliner Mid-size corporate Jet

Ruschmeyer R 90 Four seat high performance Light Aircraft

S

Saab 2000 50 seat twin Turboprop regional Airliner

Saab 340 Twin Turboprop regional Airliner

Schweizer 269/300 Light utility helicopter

Schweizer 330 Light turbine powered utility helicopter

Scorpion Homebuilt one (and later two) seater helicopter, manufactured by RotorWay International.

Scottish Aviation Jetstream 12 seat regional Turboprop Airliner

Scottish Aviation Twin Pioneer Utility Transport

Shanghai Y-10 Four-engine medium Airliner

Shorts 330 Regional Airliner and utility freighter

Shorts 360 36 seat regional Airliner

Shorts Belfast Heavy lift Turboprop freighter

Shorts Skyvan & Skyliner STOL utility Transport and regional Airliner

SIAI-Marchetti S-205/208 Four seat Light Aircraft

Sikorsky S-55 & Westland Whirlwind Mid size utility helicopter

Sikorsky S-92 Helibus Medium to heavy lift Airliner and utility helicopter

Sikorsky S-58 Mid size utility helicopter

Sikorsky S-61L & S61N Medium lift utility helicopter

Sikorsky S-62 Mid size utility helicopter

Sikorsky S-76 Mid size utility helicopter

Sino Swearingen SJ30-2 Light corporate Jet

Slingsby T-67 Firefly Two seat basic trainer

Socata GY-80 Horizon & ST-10 Diplomate Four seat Light Aircraft

Socata MS 180 & MS 250 Morane Four/ five seat Light Aircraft

Socata Rallye Series of two/four seat Light Aircraft

Socata Tangara & Gulfstream GA7 Four place Light twin

Socata TB-9/10/20/21/200 Tampico/ Tobago/Trinidad Four/five seat Light Aircraft

Socata TBM-700 Single engine corporate Turboprop

SpaceShipOne Experimental, rocket powered & glider, high altitude, suborbital

Spartan Executive 7W Single-engine radial luxury Business Aircraft of the 1930s-1940s

Sud SE-210 Caravelle Short Range Airliner

Sukhoi Su-26 Single and two seat aerobatic Light Aircraft

Su-29 Single and two seat aerobatic Light Aircraft

Su-31 Single and two seat aerobatic Light Aircraft

Sukhoi SuperJet-75 Medium Range Airliner

Sukhoi SuperJet-85 Medium Range Airliner

Sukhoi SuperJet-100 Medium Range Airliner

T

Taylorcraft series Two seat Light Aircraft

Technoavia SM92 Finist STOL utility Transport

Toyota TA-1 Prototype single engine, 4-place Aircraft

Transavia Airtruk & Skyfarmer Agricultural Aircraft

Tupolev ANT-20 "Maxim Gorky" - Largest Aircraft during the 1930s

Tupolev Tu-22

Tupolev Tu-104 Medium Range Airliner

Tupolev Tu-114 Long Range Airliner

Tupolev Tu-124 Short Range Airliner

Tupolev Tu-134 Short Range Airliner

Tupolev Tu-144 Supersonic Airliner - service withdrawn

Tupolev Tu-154 Medium Range Airliner

Tupolev Tu-204-100 Medium/Long Range Airliner

Tupolev Tu-204-120 Medium/Long Range Airliner

Tupolev Tu-204-300 Medium/Long Range Airliner

Tupolev Tu-214 Medium/Long Range Airliner

Tupolev Tu-334 Medium/Long Range Airliner

Tupolev Tu-324 Medium/Long Range Airliner

Tupolev Tu-414 Medium Range Airliner

Tupolev Tu-444 supersonic Business Jets (proposed)

V

Vickers VC10 Medium to long Range Airliner

Vickers Viscount Turboprop Airliner and freighter

Vickers Vanguard Turboprop Airliner

Victa Aircruiser Four seat Light Aircraft

Victa Airtourer Two seat Light Aircraft

VisionAire Vantage Entry level single engine corporate Jet

W

Weatherly 201/620 Agricultural Aircraft

White Knight Experimental Jet; high altitude; carry & launch smaller craft

Y

Yakovlev Yak-18T Four seat Light Aircraft

Yakovlev Yak-40 Regional Jet Airliner

Yakovlev Yak-42 Short Range Airliner

Yakovlev Yak-52 Two seat Light training Aircraft

Yunshuji 5 Chinese variation of Antonov An-2

Yunshuji 7 Chinese variation of Antonov An-24

Yunshuji 8 Chinese variation of Antonov An-12

Yunshuji 10 Chinese variation of Boeing 707 - Development program aborted.

Yunshuji 12 Chinese variation of De Havilland Canada DHC-6 Twin Otter

Z

Zivko Edge 540 Unlimited competition aerobatics Aircraft

Zlin Trener & Akrobat One and two seat aerobatic and training Light Aircraft

Zlin Z 42, Z 43, Z 142, Z 242 & Z 143 Two/four seat Light Aircraft

Aero A.10 Bi Plane five Passenger Airliner

Airbus A320 Short to medium Range Airliner

Airbus A380 Long Range high capacity Widebody Airliner

Antonov An-140 Turboprop Airliner

Avro 748 Turboprop Airliner

Beechcraft Model 55, Light Business twin

Boeing 737 medium Range narrowbody Airliner

Boeing 777-200 Long and ultra long Range Widebody Airliners

Bombardier LearJet corporate Jet

Cessna 172 Skyhawk

Cessna 208 Caravan Grand Caravan Turboprop utility Transport

De Havilland Canada DHC-1 Chipmunk Two seat Light Aircraft

Diamond DA20 Two seat Light Aircraft and basic trainer

Dornier Do 28 STOL utility Transports

Embraer ERJ 135 37 seat regional Jet Airliner

Fokker F100 100 seat regional Jet

Gulfstream American GA-7 Cougar four place Light twin-engined Aircraft

Lockheed L-1011 TriStar 500 Long Range Widebody Airliner

McDonnell Douglas DC-10 Medium to long Range Widebody Airliner

Piper PA-28 Cherokee Series Two and four seat Light Aircraft

Saab 2000 50 Seat twin Turboprop regional Airliner

Tupolev Tu-154 Medium Range Airliner

Yakovlev Yak-40 Regional Jet Airliner

Zlin Trener One and two seat aerobatic and training Light Aircraft

Courtesy: World of Civil Aircrafts by Aditi Lala and Shekhar Gupta

http://a-world-of-aviation.blogspot.ca/

www.A-World-of-Aviation.blogspot.com

Airline Codes

Airlines with Codes that begin with a number are listed in numerical order in the "Numbers" section. Codes that include a number, but start with a letter, are Listed Alphabetically in the main portion of the List.

A4 - Southern Winds - Argentina - Buenos Aires to points in Argentina, and Madrid to points in Spain and Europe

A6 - Asia Pacific Airlines - Guam - Cargo B727 in the Pacific southwest

AA - American Airlines - USA - Major Carrier

AB - Air Berlin - Germany - Flights to Palma de Mallorca and other European destiNations

AC - Air Canada - The Nation's largest Airline.

AE - Mandarin Airlines - Taiwan - Flights to Sydney, Brisbane, Auckland and Vancouver. Non-English website

AF - Air France - English site for the USA

AG - Provincial Airlines - Canada - Newfoundland and eastern Canada on Pipers and FAirchilds

AH - Air Algerie - Algeria - Flights from Frankfurt and Berlin

AI - Air India - The National Carrier

AK - AirAsia - Malaysia - 737s out of Subang

AM - Aeromexico - One of Mexico's major interNationals

AM - Island Airlines - USA - Scheduled service between Nantucket and Hyannis

AN - Ansett Australia - Died March 4, 2002

AN - Skywest - Australia - Extensive Domestic routes in western Australia. Based in Perth

AP - Air One - Italy - Lufthansa's Italian partner

AQ - Aloha Airlines - USA - The Hawaiian Islands

AR - Aerolíneas Argentinas - Argentina

AS - Alaska Airlines/Horizon Air - USA - The Western United States and Canada

AS - Horizon Air/Alaska Airlines - USA - The northwest, out of SEA-TAC and Portland

AT - Royal Air Maroc - Morocco - 747s from Montreal and JFK to Casablanca

AU - Austral Líneas Aéreas - Argentina - Twenty-four dometic destiNations

AWC - Titan Airways - UK - Corporate charters based at Stansted

AWS - Royal Wings - Jordan - Scheduled flights from Amman to Haifa, Tel Aviv, Gaza
        and Aqaba, plus charters

AY - FinnAir - Finland - Flying out of Helsinki for more than 75 years

AY - FinnAir - Finland - Official homepage for the Americas

AZ - Alitalia - Italy - Flag Carrier flies to 57 countries

B - AirBaltic - Latvia - The National Airline and SAS partner

B2 - Belavia Belarusian Airlines - Scheduled and charter flights to Europe and Asia

B3 - Bellview Airlines - Nigeria - Domestic routes on DC-9s plus NAirobi, Bombay and
        Amsterdam on an A300

B4 - Bhoja Air - Pakistan - Passenger and cargo service

B6 - JetBlue - USA - Low-fare flights on A320s

BA - British Airways - UK - "The World's Favourite Airline"

BA - GB Airways - Gibraltar - British Airways franchise flies B737s to Manchester and
        London Gatwick

BC - Air Jet - France - Commuter service between Paris and London

BD - British Midland - UK - Heathrow's second-largest operator

BG - Biman Air - Bangladesh - Asian and European capitals on DC-10s, A310s, F28s and
        BAe-ATPs

BHA - Buddha Air - Nepal - Domestic flights from Kathmandu using four Beech 1900D
        Aircraft

BI - Royal Brunei Airlines - Brunei - Southeast Asia, Australia, the Persian Gulf and the
        UK, from headquarters in Bandar Seri Begawan

BL - Pacific Airlines - Vietnam - Domestic flights, plus Taipei and Hong Kong

BO - Bouraq Airlines - Indonesia - Domestic Airline centered in Jakarta

BQ - Aeromar - Mexico - Short hops using ATR-42s

BR - EVA Air - Taiwan - The Airline arm of the Evergreen Group

BT - Air Baltic - Latvia - Flag Carrier flies to Eastern European capitals. An SAS partner

BT - Air Liberte Guadeloupe - A British Airways subsidiary

BTL - Baltia Air Lines - USA - JFK to St. Petersburg, Russia

BU - Braathens - Norway - The country's largest. Also serves Sweden

BU - Sun Air - South Africa - Flights between Johannesburg, Cape Town and Durban

BW - BWIA British West Indian - Trinidad & Tobago - L1011s and MD-83s

BX - Coast Air - Norway - Primarily operates flights between Haugesund and Bergen

BY - Britannia Airways - UK - Holiday destiNations from Germany and the UK

BZ - Keystone Air Service - Canada - Pipers and Beechcraft provide scheduled service
connecting Swan River, Dauphin and Winnipeg, Manitoba

C6 - CanJet - Canada - 737-200s on Domestic flights in eastern Canada

C8 - Chicago Express Airlines - USA - An American Trans Air connector.

CA - Air China - The largest operator within the People's Republic

CB - Scot Airways - Scotland - Used to be Suckling Airways

CC - Air Atlanta Icelandic - A privately-owned contract Carrier

CC - MacAir Airlines - Australia - Saabs, FAirchilds and Otters in Queensland

CD - Mindanao Express Airlines - Philippines - Connects Mindanao with the rest of the
Philippines

CE - Nationwide Airlines - South Africa - B727s, B737s and B767s on Domestic flights
plus London Gatwick

CG - MBA Milne Bay Airlines - Papua New Guinea - More than 400 scheduled and
charter Domestic flights per week

CI - China Airlines - World destiNations fanning out from Taipei

CJ - China Northern Airlines - Extensive Domestic system using A300, MD-90 and MD-
82 Aircraft

CJ - Colgan Air - USA - Continental Connctions on the eastern seaboard

CL - Lufthansa CityLine - Germany - Five hundred flights a day to 61 European cities. CRJs and Avros

CM - COPA - Panama - Fifteen 737s out of Panama City's Tocumen InterNational Airport

CN - Tropic Air - Belize - Eight Domestic flights, plus Flores (Tikal), Guatemala

CO - Continental Airlines - USA - Major Carrier

CU- Cubana - Cuba - Domestic flights, plus Europe, South America and Canada

CV - Cargolux - Luxembourg - Seven 747-400Fs Fly cargo to every continent except Australia

CX - Cathay Pacific - Hong Kong - 747s, 777s, A330s and A340s

CY - Cyprus Airways

CZ - China Southern Airlines - Boeings serving China and southeast Asia

D3 - Daallo Airlines - Djibouti/Somalia - AN-24s, IL-18s and TU-154s

DA - Air Georgia - Georgia - Flies between Tblisi and Frankfurt

DB - Brit Air - France - A regional arm of Air France

DD - Nok Air - Thailand - Low-cost Airline with service from Bangkok to Chiang Mai, Hat Yai and Udon Thani

DE - Condor - Germany - North American site for this German holiday service

DL - Delta - USA - Major Carrier

DL - Delta Express - USA - The eastern states to Florida

DL - Song - USA - Delta's low cost Carrier

DM - Maersk Air - Denmark - From Copenhagen and Brillund to major European cities

DP - Air 2000 - UK - Scheduled and chartered holiday flights

DP - First Choice - UK - Holiday flights to Southern Europe, Northern Africa and the Caribbean

DS - Air Senegal - Senegal - Member of the Groupe Royal Air Maroc. Three B737s and a Dash 8

DU - Hemus Air - Bulgaria - From Sofia to Europe, Africa and the Near East

DV - Nantucket Airlines - USA - Back and forth between Hyannis and Nantucket every hour

DW - Rottnest Air Taxi - Australia - Connects Rottnest Island with Freemantle

DWT - Darwin Airline - Switzerland - SAAB 2000s between Lugano, Geneva, Barcelona and Olbia

DX - DanAir - UK - An unofficial, commemorative site. Taken over by BA in '93

DZ - Transcaraibes Air InterNational/Air Tropical - Guadeloupe - Island hopping in the French West Indies

E5 - Samara Airlines - Russia - Domestic flights on Tupolevs, Ilushyns, Yakolevs and Antonovs

E8 - AlpiEagles - Italy - Domestic and interNational

ED - CCAir (US Airways Express) - USA - Charlotte, NC to 25 cities in 8 states

EI - Aer Lingus - Ireland's National Airline

EJ - New England Airlines - USA - From Westerly, RI to Block Island twelve times a day and more

EK - Emirates - UAE - Based in Dubai, the flag Carrier uses Airbuses and 777s

EM - Western Airlines - Australia - Flies from Perth to Geraldton, Kalbarri, Denham and Monkey Mia

EN - Air Dolomiti - Italy -Flights to Switzerland, Germany and Spain on ATRs and CRJs. A Lufthansa partner

EP - Europe Airpost - France - Formerly Aéropostale

EQ - TAME - Ecuador

ET - Ethiopian Airlines - Domestic flights, plus Europe, Africa, Middle East and Asia

EW - Eurowings - Germany - Regional flights throughout Europe

EZ - Sun Air - Denmark - Jetstreams between Sweden, Norway, Ireland and Germany

F3 - Flying Enterpise - Sweden - Stockholm, Skövde, Jönköping and Visby

F4 - Eureca - Italy - Domestic flights in northern Italy on Fokkers and a FAirchild Metroliner

FA - SafAir - South Africa - Passenger and cargo flights with 727s, MD80s and Hercules L382Gs

FB - Fine Air - USA - Cargo flights to South and Central America and Caribbean

FF - Tower Air - USA - Select US and European destiNations from their terminal at JFK

FG - Ariana Afghan Airlines - Afghanistan - The Middle East plus Moscow, Frankfurt and Istanbul

FI - IcelandAir - Iceland - Europe and North America from Keflavik

FJ - Air Pacific - Fiji - One B747, one B767 and three B737s with an average age of seven
    years

FL - AirTran Airways - USA - Atlanta to the mid- and eastern US on B717s

FL - Frontier Airlines - USA - Domestic flights centered in Denver

FM - Shanghai Airlines - China - Boeing 737s, 757s, and 767s to major Asian and
    European destiNations

FO - Expedition Airways - Zimbabwe - Seven Zimbabwe destiNations, plus South Africa
    and Mozambique using a Beechcraft 1900C

FP - Par Avion Airlines - Australia - Operates in Tasmania

FQ - Air Aruba - To Aruba from Columbia, the US and Sao Paulo

FQ - Thomas Cook Airlines - Belgium - From Belgium to European holiday spots

FR - RyanAir - Ireland - Budget flights from Dublin to Europe on twenty-two 737s

FS - Staf Cargo Airlines - USA - DC-10 and 747 freighters from Miami to South America

FT - Vancouver Island Air - Canada - Beech seaplanes and deHavilland Beavers from
    Campbell River, BC

FU - Air Littoral - France - CRJs and ATR 42-500s out of Montpellier and Nice

G1 - Gorkha Airlines - Nepal - Eight Domestic destiNations

G3 - Emerald Airways - UK - Cargo flights in BAe 748 and Shorts SD360 out of Liverpool's
    John Lennon

G4 - Allegiant Air - USA - Domestic DC-9 service

G5 - Island Air - Cayman Islands - Scheduled service to Cayman Brac and Little Cayman,
    plus charters and sightseeing tours

G7 - Gandalf Airlines - Italy - From Milan to major European capitals in FAirchild-
    Dornier 328s

G9 - Air Arabia - UAE - Based in Sharjah, with flights throughout the Middle East on
    A320s

GA - Citilink - Indonesia - Garuda Indonesia's low-cost Domestic service. B737s.

GA - Garuda Indonesia - Indonesia - Extensive Domestic and interNational network

GF - Gulf Air - Has four owner states: Bahrain, Oman, Qatar and UAE

GH - Ghana Airways - Flights to and from West Africa and Accra

GL - Air Greenland - Domestic flights, plus Denmark

GM - Air Slovakia - Slovakia - B737s from Slovensko to the Mediterranean

GQ - BigSky Airlines - USA - Short hops west of the Mississippi

GS - AirFoyle - UK - Cargo and scheduled passenger service

GT - Air Mandalay - Myanmar - Domestic Airline

GU - Riga Airlines - Latvia - London, Moscow and Paris to Riga

GX - Air Ontario - Canada - Regional Airline for the Great Lakes and north eastern US.
Folded into parent company Air Canada's regional line: Jazz

GY - Guyana Airways

H2 - City Bird - Belgium - Brussels to the US, Mexico and Europe

HA - Hawaiian Airlines - USA - All Hawaiian islands and west coast USA

HF - Hapag-Lloyd - Germany - Extensive network of European holiday destiNations
using A310s and B737s

HH - Islandsflug - Iceland - Domestic flights on B737s, ATR-42s, Dornier 228s and a
Piper Chieftan

HK - Yangon Airways - Myanmar - Regional Airline

HM - Air Seychelles - Seychelles - From European and African capitals to the Indian
Ocean paradise

HP - America West Airlines - USA - Hubbed in Arizona

HQ - HMY Airways - Canada - B757s between Vancouver and Toronto

HR - Hahn Air - Germany - Charters on FAirchilds and SAABs

HSA - East African Safari Air - Kenya - France and Italy to NAirobi, plus charters

HV - Transavia - Netherlands - Amsterdam to Eurpoean holiday spots

HY - Uzbekistan Airways - From Tashkent to Asia and Europe

IB - Iberia - Spain - The flag Carrier

IC - Indian Airlines - India - Wholly owned by the Government of India

IE - Solomon Airlines - Solomon Islands - To Australia and neighbouring islands on
B737s, three Islanders, and two Twin Otters

IG - Meridiana - Italy - Low-cost Carrier to Domestic points plus Madrid, Barcelona and Amsterdam

IM - Spirit Airlines - USA - Flights between Florida and the northeast

IR - Iran Air - Tehran to Europe and Asia, plus Domestic flights

IV - WindJet - Italy - Low-cost flights throughtout Italy and to select European cities

IY - Yemenia Airways - Yemen - From Sana'a to 25 cities in Europe, the Middle East and Africa

IY - Yemenia Airways - Yemen - Unofficial North-American site

IZ - Arkia Israeli Airlines - Vacation charters within Israel

J4 - Buffalo Airways - Canada - Charter work on a variety of Aircraft. Based in Yellowknife, NWT

JA - Air Bosna - Bosnia and Herzegovina - One ATR-42, two YAK-42s and a Cessna 550 to Eastern Europe and Scandanavia

JB - Helijet Airways - Canada - Scheduled helicopters: Vancouver, Victoria and Seattle

JD - Japan Air System - Ninety-nine Domestic rutes

JE - Manx Airlines - UK - From the Isle of Man to Ireland, Scotland and England

JF - L.A.B. Flying Service - USA - Daily scheduled flights connecting Haines, Alaska with Juneau, Skagway and other S.E. Alaska communities

JL - Japan Airlines - Tokyo and Osaka to all major world destiNations

JM - Air Jamaica - Montego Bay to the US and the Caribbean

JP - Adria Airways - Slovenia

JU - JAT Yugoslav Airlines - Unofficial site, but good enough to warrant an exception

JV - Bearskin Airlines - Canada - Serving Northern Ontario

JX - SunJet - USA - Twenty daily flights between New York and Florida

JY - British European Airways - UK - Domestic flights, including Jersey and Guernsey

K5 - Wings of Alaska - USA - Cessnas, Beavers and Otters out of Juneau

KA - Dragon Air - Hong Kong - Southeast Asia regional Airline

KB - Druk Air (Royal Bhutan Airlines) - Bhutan - India, Nepal, Bhutan, Thailand

KD - Kendell Airlines - Australia

KE - Korean Air - Southeast Asia plus select European and North Amercan cities

KF - Air Botnia - Finland - now Blue1, a subsidiary of SAS. Third largest regional Airline in Europe

KF - Blue1 - Finland - formerly Air Botnia, a subsidiary of SAS. Third largest regional Airline in Europe

KK - TAM - Brazil - An A319, A330s, Fokkers and Caravans

KL - KLM Royal Dutch Airlines - Netherlands - Schiphol to major world destiNations

KM - Air Malta - To Europe and the Middle East

KQ - Kenya Airways - NAirobi to the rest of Africa and select world destiNations

KS - PenAir (Peninsula Airways) - USA - Thirty-five small Aircraft to 73 communites. An Alaska Airlines partner

KU - Kuwait Airways - Forty destiNations

KX - Cayman Airways - Cayman Islands to Florida, Texas and Jamaica

L2 - Lynden Air Cargo - USA - Hercs hauling oversize loads in Alaska

LA - LanChile Airlines - South, Central and North America, some Australia, some Europe

LB - Albanian Airlines - Albania - three Aircraft serving destiNations in Italy, Turkey, Germany, Switzerland and Kosovo together with a growing charter programme

LB - Lloyd Aero Boliviano - Bolivia

LC - LoganAir - UK - Serving Scotland for British Airways

LG - LuxAir - Luxembourg - 737s, Embraers and Fokkers to the rest of Europe, North Africa and New York

LH - Lufthansa - Germany's biggest and most famous

LH - Lufthansa Cargo - Germany - The flag Carrier's freight division

LI - LIAT - Antigua - Two hundred flights a day in the eastern Caribbean

LM - Air ALM (Antillean Airlines) - Venezuela to the Caribbean and southeast United States

LN - Libyan Arab Airlines - Libya

LO - LOT Polish Airlines - Dates back to the 1920s

LP - LanPreu - Peru - Peruvian arm of an extensive worldwide Airline

LT - LTU InterNational Airways - Germany - Holiday destiNations in Florida, California and the Caribbean

LW - Pacific Wings Hawaii - USA - Island hopping in hawaii with Cessna 402Cs

LX - Swiss InterNational Airlines - Switzerland - Worldwide destiNations. Was CrossAir

LY - El Al - Israel - Flag Carrier flies from Tel Aviv to the world

LZ - Balkan Bulgarian Airlines - Bulgarian flag Carrier uses Tupolevs, Antonovs and 737s

M2 - Southeast Air Freight - Bahamas - Daily scheduled freight service between Nassau and Freeport

M3 - European Air Express - Germany - Business commuter flights out of Cologne/Bonn

M3 - WestJet - Canada - Twelve 737s serve 11 cities in western Canada

M4 - Avioimpex - Macedonia - From Skopje to Istanbul and major european capitals on DC-9s and MD-80s

M7 - MAT Macedonian Airlines - Macedonia

MA - Malev Hungarian - Based at Budapest's Ferihegy InterNational Airport

MD - Air Madagascar - Eastern Africa's premiere Air service

ME - MEA Middle East Airlines - Lebanon - Airbuses to Europe and the Middle East

MF - Xiamen Airlines - China - Thiry-seven Boeings Fly an extensive Domestic network

MH - Malaysia Airlines - 110 destiNations on 6 continents

MI - Silk Air - Singapore - This regional wing of Singapore Airlines flies A320s

MK - Air Mauritius - Flag Carrier flies from the island Nation to Africa, Asia, Australia and Eurpoe

ML - Midway Airlines - USA - Raleigh-Durham to the rest of the eastern seaboard on B737s, CRJs and Fokker F100s

MN - British Airways South Africa - Operated by ComAir

MO - Calm Air - Canada - Canadian InterNational partner serves Ontario, Manitoba and Nunavut

MP - MartinAir - Netherlands

MS - EgyptAir - 95 destiNations on a fleet with an average age of 6 years

MU - China Eastern Air - Based in Shanghai's Hongqiao InterNational Airport

MW - Maya Airways - Belize - Nine Domestic destiNations

MW - Maya Island Air - Belize - From Ambergris Caye to the rest of Belize, plus Mexico and Guatemala

MX - Mexicana - Mexico City to major North American and South American cities

MY - Euroscot - Scotland - Domestic regional Airline. Now operated by Gill Air

N6 - Aero Continente - Peru - Extensive Domestic routes

NB - National Airlines - USA - Las Vegas to Los Angeles, San Francisco, Chicago-Midway and JFK

NB - Sterling - Denmark - Low-cost flight from Copenhagen and Stockholm to Mediterranean hotspots

NG - Lauda Air - Austria - The famous F1 driver spawned an Airline

NH - All Nippon Airways - Japan - Flights to both US seaboards

NI - PGA Portugalia Airlines - Portugal - Fokker 100s and Embraer 145s to Europe and the Grand Canary Islands

NI - Portugália Airlines - Portugal - From Lisbon to Spain, Germany, France, Italy, Belgium, and the UK with Fokkers 100s and Embraer 145s

NJ - Vanguard Airlines - USA - Ten Domestic destiNations

NL - Shaheen Air InterNational - Pakistan - Karachi, Islamabad, Lahore and Peshawar, plus Abu Dhabi, Dubai, Kuwait, Alain and Muscat

NN - Cardinal Airlnes - USA - Melborne, FL to Baltimore/Washington on MD-80s

NO - Aus-Air - Australia - Regional flights to the southern islands

NP - Skytrans Airlines - Australia - Various small Aircraft perform scheduled and charter duties in Queensland

NR - SpanAir - Spain - Domestic flights plus major South American and European destiNations

NW - Northwest Airlines - USA - Major Carrier soon to be Flying out of its Detroit Midfield Terminal

NW - Pacific Island Aviation - Northern Mariana Islands - Operates flights for Northwest Airlines, connecting the islands of Guam, Rota, Tinian and Saipan

NX - Air Macau - Five A321s and three A320s serve China and S.E. Asia

NY - Air Iceland - Domestic flights plus Greenland

NZ - Air New Zealand - Flag Carrier

OA - Olympic Airways - Greece - Flag Carrier

OG - Go - UK - Now easyjet.

OH - ComAir - USA - Delta Connections using more than 70 CanadAir Regionals

OK - Czech Airlines - Czech Republic - From Prague to world destiNations

OL - OLT - Germany - Commuter flights from Bremen to London, Berlin, Naples, Toulouse

OM - MIAT Mongolian Airlines - Domestic service plus Moscow, Berlin and southeast
    Asia, using ANs, an A310 and three 727s

ON - Air Nauru - Nauru to Australia, Fiji, Kiribati, and the Solomon Islands

OP - Chalk's Ocean Airways - USA - Miami and Ft. Lauderdale to the Bahamas on
    Grumman G-73T Turbine Millard amphibious Aircraft

OS - Austrian Airlines - A SwissAir partner

OU - Croatia Airlines - The National Airline based in Zagreb

OV - Estonian Air - To major western European capitals

OX - Orient Thai Airlines - Thailand - Southeast Asia on B747s and L1011s

OZ - Asiana Airlines - S. Korea - From Kimpo InterNational to Asian destiNations

P8 - Pantanal Linhas Aéreas - Brazil - Domestic flights from Sao Paulo on an ATR-42

PA - Pan Am - USA - The latest incarNation

PA -Pan American World Airways - USA - This site commemorates this now-defunct
    major Carrier

PC - Air Fiji - Domestic Airline with 65 flights a day

PD - Trillium Air - Canada - Serving Kitchener and Ottawa with Jetstream 31/Super31s

PF - Palestinian Airlines - One Fokker 50 and one 727 from Gaza to Amman, CAiro,
    Dubai and Jeddah

PG - Bangkok Airways - Thailand - Flights from Bangkok to Thai resorts plus Phnom-
    Penh

PH - Polynesian Airlines - Samoa - National Carrier connects the south Pacific to Australia
    and the US

PI - Piedmont Airlines - USA - US Airways Express

PK - Pakistan InterNational Airlines - Flag Carrier

PR - Philippine Airlines

PS - Ukraine InterNational Airlines - Jointly owned by the government, SwissAir and the GPA Group, Inc.

PW - Precision Air - Tanzania - Scheduled, charter and scenic flights out of Arusha, Dar es Salaam and Bukoba

PX - Air Niugini - Papua New Guinea - The National Airline

PY - Surinam Airways - Surinam

Q2 - Minerva Airlines - Italy - Partner to Alitalia

Q3 - Roan Air - Zambia - Domestic flights, with plans for London and Johannesburg

Q4 - Mustique Airways - St. Vincent and the Grenadines - Island hopping in the Eastern Caribbean

Q7 - Sobel Air - Belgium - A charter remnant of Sabena

QA - Aerocaribe - Mexico - A regional arm of Mexicana

QAH - Quick Airways - Netherlands - Rotterdam and Groningen

QF - Qantas Airways - The Australian leader, and tenth largest in the world

QF - Southern Australia Airlines - Qantas-owned regional Airline based in Victoria

QK - Air Nova- Canada - Atlantic coast regional arm of Air Canada. Folded into parent company Air Canada's regional line: Jazz

QP - Airkenya - Kenya - Domestic flights

QQ - Reno Air - USA - Commemorative website. Purchased by American Airlines in 1999

QR - Qatar Airways - From Doha to the rest of the Middle East

R6 - Air Srpska - Republic of Srpska - An ATR72-202, leased from JAT Yugoslavia, flies between Banja Luka and Zurich

R7 - Aserca Airlines - Venezuela - Domestic and interNational flights

RA - Royal Nepal - Kathmandu to select European and East Asian cities

RB - SyrianAir - Syria - A320s, B727s and B747s to major European and Middle East capitals

RE - Aer Arann Express - Ireland - Regional Airline connects the Aran Islands with Dublin and the rest of the Republic

RC - Atlantic Airways - Faroe Islands - Two BAe-200s and a Bell Helicopter from the islands to Iceland, the UK, Norway and Denmark

RG - VARIG Airlines - Brazil - The Nation's first Airline dates back to the '20s

RI - Mandala Airlines - Indonesia - Domestic flights

RJ - Royal Jordanian - Jordan - Airbuses from Amman to the Middle East and Europe

RK - Air Afrique - Connecting Europe and West Africa

RO - TAROM - Romanian Air Transport - Flag Carrier flies to major world destiNations

RQ - Air Engiadina - Switzerland - Regional Airline using Dornier 328s

RT - Airlines of South Australia - Regional Airline boasts "The World's Longest Mail Run"

RYN - Ryan InterNational Airlines - USA - Holiday destiNations from Kansas City, plus cargo for Emery Worldwide

RZ - Sansa - Costa Rica - One of Grupo Taca's regional Airlines. Fifteen Domestic destiNations

S2 - Sahara India Airlines - India - Domestic Airline flies B737-400s and helicopters

S5 - Shuttle America - USA - Dash 8s in the northeast US

S7 - Siberia Airlines - Russia - InterNational and Domestic service on Tupolevs and Ilushyns

SA - South African Airways - Flag Carrier

SB - Aircalin - New Caledonia - Domestic flights and some southwest Pacific destiNations

SB - TIE - Trans InterNational Express - USA - From JFK to Albany, NY, New Haven, CT and Binghampton, NY

SC - Shandong Airline - China - Domestic flights on 737s and SAAB-340s

SD - Sudan Airways - Sudan - B707s, B737s and an A300

SE - SeAir - Philippines - A complete Domestic schedule, plus an amphibean Dornier DO-24 for charter

SG - Sempati Air - Indonesia - A Fokker 70

SJ - Polar Air Cargo - USA - Scheduled worldwide freight service on B747s

SK - SAS - Sweden - Boeings and MDs to North America, Europe and Asia

SK - Skyline Airways - Nepal - Domestic flights

SL - Rio-Sul - Brazil - Domestic Carrier

SLI - Aerolitoral - Mexico - A regional Airline

SN - Sabena - Website details the Airline's bankruptcy

SN - SN Brussels Airline - Belgium - The new National Airline

SO - Swiss World - Switzerland - Geneva to Montreal, Newark and Miami

SP - SATA - Portugal - Includes Sata Air Acores, Sata Internacional, Sata Express and Azores Express

SP - Sata Air Açores - Portugal - Flights between the islands, and to Toronto, Boston, Lisbon, Porto and Madeira

SQ - Singapore Airlines - 747s and 777s to world destiNations

SS - CorsAir - France - Holiday destintions in the US, Africa and Thailand

SSV - Skyservice - Canada - From Toronto to holiday destiNations

SU - Aeroflot - Russia's interNational Airline

SV - Saudi Arabian Airlines - 126 planes connect the Arabian Peninsula to major world destiNations

SW - Air Namibia

SY - Sun Country Airlines - USA - Low fares from Minneapolis/St. Paul to holiday destiNations, plus charters

SZ - China Southwest Airlines - China - Extensive list of Domestic destiNations

SZ - Pro Air - USA - Four 737s Flying from Detroit to eight destiNations

T4 - Transeast Airlines - Latvia - From Riga to Jonkoping and Billund

TA - TACA (Grupo Taca) - El Salvador - Lima, San Jose and San Salvador to the Americas

TC - Air Tanzania - Tanzania - Dubai, Johannesburg, Muscat, NAirobi, Mombasa and Zanzibar, plus many destiNations within Tanzania

TE - Lithuanian Airlines - From Vilnius to northern Eurpoean capitals on B737s and SAABs

TG - Thai Airways InterNational - A large and varied fleet

TK - Turkish Airlines - Flag Carrier

TL - Airnorth - Australia - Largest regional operator in Northern Australia

TL - Trans Mediterranean Airways - Lebannon - Cargo flights on six B707s

TM - LAM Linhas Aéreas de Mocambique - Mozambique

TN - Air Tahiti Nui - Tahiti

TP - TAP Air Portugal - 737s and most of the Airbus family

TPC - Air Caladonie - New Caledonia - Dornier, ATR 42 and AT4 Aircraft make frequent
    Domestic trips

TR - TransBrasil - 737s and 767s on Domestic flights, plus some USA and Europe

TS - Air Transat - Canada - Discount charter and scheduled flights

TT - Air Lithuania - Lithuania - Mostly business flights around Norther Europe

TU - TunisAir - Tunisia - Forty-seven flights a day to major European capitals

TV - Virgin Express - Belgium - Commuter/feeder Airline links ten European cities

TW - Trans World Airlines: TWA - USA - Major Domestic Carrier with world destiNations

TX - Air Caribes - French West Indies - Eight daily round trips between St. Maarten and
    St. Barth

TZ - American Trans Air - USA - Indianapolis charter and military contracts

U2 - easyJet - UK - Budget flights on 737s from London Luton

U3 - TravelAir - Costa Rica - From San Jose to anywhere in Costa Rica in less than an
    hour

U6 - Ural Airlines - Russia - Ekaterinburg to the rest of Russia

UA - United Airlines - USA - Major interNational Carrier

UB - Myanmar Airways InterNational - Myanmar - Yangon, Bangkok, Hong Kong,
    Singapore, Kuala Lumpur

UK - KLM uk - UK - Seventeen UK Airports to Schiphol

UL - SriLankan - Sri Lanka - Flag Carrier goes to Europe, Asia and the Middle East.
    Previously AirLanka

UM - Air Zimbabwe - Flights throughout southen Africa

UN - Transaero - Russia - Russia's first privately-owned Airline flies to many major
    Russian and European cities

UP - BahamasAir - National Airline serves Florida and the Islands

US - Chautauqua Airlines (US Airways Express) - USA - Twelve SAAB-340s and 17 Jetstream-31s out of Indianapolis

US - MetroJet - USA - US Airways' partner east of the Mississippi

US - US Airways - USA - Hubs at Pittsburgh, Charlotte, Philadelphia and Baltimore-Washington

UU - Air Austral - France - The India Ocean

UW - Perimeter - Canada - Metros provide scheduled service in Manitoba and Northwestern Ontario

UX - Air Europa - Spain - Domestic holiday destiNations. An Alitalia partner

UX - Air Luxor - Portugal - Business and holiday charters on L-1011, A320 and various private-sized Aircraft

UY - Cameroon Airlines - Central Africa plus Jeddah, Paris, London and Brussels with B747 and B737

V3 - VanAir - Vanuatu - Serves 29 Airports in the archipelago

VG - VLM Airlines - Belgium - Regional flights on Fokkers

VI - Volga-Dnepr Airlines - Russia - Super-heavy cargo on AN 124-100

VL - North Vancouver Air - Canada - From Vancouver to Seattle and southern British Columbia on Beech, Pipers, J31s and a Cessna 206

VM - Regional Airlines - France - Created in 1992 by th merging ofAir Vendée with Airlec

VN - Vietnam Airlines - Europe and Asia from Hanoi and Ho Chi Minh City

VO - Tyrolean Airways - Austria - Member of the Austrian Airlines Group flies to 49 destiNations in 24 countries

VP - VASP - Brazil - MD-11s and 737s to 27 Brazilian cities and 12 interNational destiNations

VQ - Impulse Airlines - Australia - Now Jetstar, Qantas' new low-cost Carrier

VQ - Jetstar - Australia - Qantas' low-cost Carrier. Formerly Impulse Airlines

VR - Cabo Verde Airlines - Cape Verde to Boston, Amsterdam, Paris and Munich

VS - Virgin Atlantic - UK - London and Manchester to major world cities

VV - AeroSvit Airlines - Ukraine - Founded in 1994, flies B737s from Kiev to the rest of the country, plus Moscow and the Mediterranean

VV - Aerosweet - Ukraine - One of three major Carriers

VW - Skyways - Sweden - Domestic partner of SAS uses Saabs, Fokkers and Jetstreams

W3 - SwiftAir - Spain - Flies cargo for DHL

W5 - Mahan Air - Iran - Airbuses and Tu-154s to Domestic points plus select interNational cities

W6 - Wizz - UK - Nine A320s serving Central and Eastern Europe

W9 - Eastwind Airlines - USA - Greensboro and Orlando to the northeast

WC - Isleña - Honduras - One of Grupo Taca's regional Airlines. Service to the Bay Islands, Copan, and the country's interior

WF - Widerøe Airline - Norway - Extensive Domestic routes, plus seven interNational routes

WG - Wasaya Airways - Canada - Owned by eight Native Canadian communities

WJ - Air Labrador - Canada -Labrador and Newfoundland

WL - Aeroperlas - Panama - Scheduled and charter flights on Shorts, Otters, Cessnas and Beech Kings

WN - Southwest Airlines - USA - 737s to 54 Domestic destiNations

WNA - WinAir - St. Maarten - Frequent service from St. Maarten to neighbouring islands

WO - World Airways - USA - An MD-11 and a DC-10

WR - Royal Tongan Airlines - Tonga

WT - Nigeria Airlines - Nigeria - Lagos to Heathrow and JFK

WX - CityJet - UK - London and Dublin to the Costa del Sol

WY - Oman Air - Oman - InterNational flights from Muscat on B737s and ATRs

X5 - Cronus Airlines - Greece - To Greece from Germany, Rome and Paris

XG - North American Airlines - USA - 757s and MD-83s provide feeder flights to JFK for El Al

XJ - Mesaba Airlines - USA - A Northwest Airlines partner out of Minneapolis and Detroit

XP - Casino Express Airlines - USA - delivers vacationers from over 90 cities in the US to Elko, Nevada.

XZ - EastAir - Sweden - Lear Jets and Piper PA-31s based at Bromma

YB - South African Express Airways - Connector flights centered in Johannsburg

YC - Flight West - Australia - Regional Airline based in Queensland

YI - Air Sunshine - USA - Florida, Bahamas, Puerto Rico, Virgin Islands, Dominican Republic and Turks & Caicos

YK - Cyprus Turkish Airlines - North Cyprus - From Turkey and London to North Cyprus

YN - Air Creebec - Canada - Airlne owned by the Cree Nation serves northern Quebec and Ontario

YT - Skywest - USA - Brasilia EMB-120s and CanadAir Regionals out of Salt Lake City, LAX and San Francisco

YV - Mesa Air Group - USA - America West Express, US Airways Express, and Mesa Airlines

YX - Midwest Express Airlines - USA - Domestic flights on DC-9s, MD-80s and Beechcraft

Z4 - Zoom - Canada - Connects Canada and the UK with B767s

Z5 - GMG Airlines - Bangladesh - Regional flights centered in Dhaka

ZA - AccessAir - USA - 737s based in Des Moines, Iowa

ZB - Monarch Airlines - UK - Scheduled and charter flights to European holiday spots

ZI - Aigle Azur - France - Holiday flights to Algeria on A321s and B737s

ZK - Great Lakes Aviation - USA - United Express flights: Chicago Meigs and Springfield

ZK - United Express - USA - Great Lakes Aviation flights: Chicago Meigs and Springfield

ZQ - Qantas New Zealand - Domestic Airline. Previously Ansett New Zealand

ZR - Muk Air - Denmark - Short flights from Copenhagen to other Scandanavian cities

ZU - Freedom Air InterNational - New Zealand - Flights betweem New Zealand and Australia

ZW - Air Wisconsin - USA - This United Express feeder operates BAe146s, Fokkers and CanadAirs to Chicago and the west

2K - Kitty Hawk - USA - Scheduled and charter cargo flights, mostly on B727s

2M - Moldavian Airlines - Moldova - Chisinau to Budapest on SAAB 2000s

2P - Air Philippines - The country's second-largest Airline

2S - Sun Air - Fiji - Domestic flights on De Havillands and Beechcraft out of Nadi InterNational Airport

2Y - HelenAir Caribbean - St. Lucia - Frequent flights to several islands in the West Indies

3C - Corporate Express - Canada - Scheduled business flights in Alberta and British Columbia

3D - Denim Airways - Germany - Dusseldorf, Augsburg and Berlin

3H - Air Inuit - Canada - Northern Quebec

3L - InterSky - Germany - Dash 8 flights connect major German cities, plus Bern and Vienna

3M - Continental Connection (Gulfstream) - USA

3R - Air Moldova InterNational - Republic of Moldova to Europe and Russia

3S - Air Antilles - Guyana - Low-fare, no-frills subsidiary of Air Guyane

3S - Shuswap Air - Canada - Charters a Beech King from Salmon Arm, BC

3U - Sichuan Airlines - China - Connects Sichuan province to the rest of China

3Z - Necon Air - Nepal - Domestic flights plus northern India on Avro HS-748s, an ATR-42 and a Cessna Caravan

4L - Air Alma - Canada - A Canadian InterNational partner

4N - Air North - Canada - B737 service Calgary/Edmonton to Whitehorse and Vancouver/Whitehorse; Hawker Siddeley 748 service between Whitehorse and Dawson City, Old Crow, Inuvik (NWT), plus FAirbanks & Juneau

4V - Voyageur Airways - Canada - Ski charters in Ontario and Quebec

4Y - Yute Air - USA - From Dillingham to western Alaska

4Z - South African Airlink - South Africa - Embraers and Jetstreams feed the parent Airline

5F - Arctic Circle Air Service - USA - scheduled passenger and freight service from hubs in Aniak, Bethel, Dillingham and FAirbanks, Alaska

5J - Cebu Pacific Air - Philippines - Twelve DC-9s make Domestic flights out of Manila

5K - Kenmore Air - USA - Scheduled seaplane flights: Seattle, Victoria, San Juan Isl.

5U - Skagway Air Service - USA - Daily flights between Juneau and Skagway, Alaska

5Y - Atlas Air - USA - Twenty-nine cargo B747s

6A - Aviacsa Airlines - Mexico - Extensive Domestic routes, plus Houston and Las Vegas

6E - Malmo Aviation - Sweden - Malmo and Umea to Stockholm Bromma on Avros and BAes

6N - Nordic Leisure - Sweden - Charters on MD-80s

6N - TTA TransTravel - Netherlands - A Dash-8 and a Beech between Rotterdam, Hamburg, Göteborg and Copenhagen

6P - Club Air - Italy - From Verona to Eastern Europe

6Q - Slovak Airlines - Slovakia - TU-154 and B737 service from Bratislava to Brussels and Moscow

6U - Air Ukraine Cargo - Ukraine - Cargo division of AeroSvit flies a B767 four time a week between JFK and Kiev

6V - Air Vegas - USA Sightseeing tours of the Grand Canyon

7A - Haines/Alaska Coastal Airways - USA - Short hops in southeast Alaska

7B - KrasAir-Krasnoyarsk Airlines - Russia - Extensive Domestic and European network on Tuploevs and Illushyns

7C - Coyne Airways - Russia - Scheduled cargo and passenger flights in the Caspian Sea area

7F - First Air - Canada - Connecting Canada's north and far north

7G - Gulfstream Airlines - USA - "Continental Connection" in the southeast states

7L - AB Airlines - UK - London Gatwick to Nice, Shannon and Barcelona

7P - Batavia Air - Indonesia - Domestic flights on B737s and Dash 200s

7V - Austin Express - USA - Texas flights in a FAirchild Metroliner

7Y - West Isle Air - USA - Cessnas serving the San Juan Islands

8D - Volareweb - Italy - Low-cost arm of Volare Airlines

8E - Bering Air - USA - Alaskan Air taxi

8G - Angel Air - Thailand - Unofficial site for this Domestic Airline

8H - Harbour Air - Canada - Scheduled seaplane flights from Vancouver

8M - MaxAir - Sweden - Flights connecting Malmö, Sweden with Hamburg, Germany and Oslo, Norway

8O - West Coast Air - Canada - Twin Otter service between Victoria's Inner Harbour and Vancouver's Coal Harbour

8P - Pacific Coastal Airlines - Canada - A Canadian partner serving the southern coast of British Columbia

8U - Afriqiyah Airways - Libya - A320s based in Tripoli and going to Europe and N. Africa

8W - BAX Global (Burlington Air Express) - USA - Cargo flights to Canada, the US and Mexico on DC-8s and B727s

9C - Wimbi Dira Airways - Congo - Domestic flights out of Kinshasa

9K - Cape Air - USA - Cape Cod, Key West, the Caribbean and the Outer Banks

9M - Central Mountain Air - Canada - Air Canada's regional partner flies Beechcraft 1900Ds

9N - Trans States Airlines - USA - Jetstreams serving 53 US cities

9T - Transwest Air - Canada - Manitoba and Saskatchewan. Previously Athabaska Air

9W - Jet Airways - India - Thirty Domestic destiNations using 737s

9Y - Air Kazakstan - National Carrier flies to Europe and Asia

Books by AeroSoft from the same Author

P - Productivity S - Speed R - Relevancy

Price: $20.00 USD. Approx. 22,870 words. Language: English.

Category: Essay.

How to Take Off Your Professional **Career** from an Average to Exceptional with the Hidden PSR in You. A Book By working CEO and Manager with Day to day and live Examples How to Fight with Global Recession.**By Shekhar Gupta Surbhi Maheshwari**

Published: Aug. 23, 2013

Words: 22,870 (approximate)

Language: English

ISBN: 9781301432448

Be An Aviator not A Pilot

Be an Aviator Not a Pilot is a story of Pilots in Aviation who are unable to cope. This is not a book to teach you how to get into an Aviation School or even how to live like a Pilot. In fact, it describes how one can become a Successfull Aviator not just an Airplane Driver [So called Pilot] with very small changes in life. Also Why abroad trained Pilots are better Aviator and Why FAA, CASA, CAAP, CAA are better civil Aviation Authority then DGCA. **By Shekhar Gupta and Ankisha Awasthi**

Price:$1.99 USD.

Words: 4,750 (approximate)

Language: English.

Published on July 24, 2013.

Category: Fiction. As A Fact Out Of Every 1000 Pilots Only 1 Pilot Becomes An **Airline** Pilot, The Book Is All About Those 999 Pilots Only.

Cabin Crew Career Guide

Category: Essay >>Literature

Published: Sept. 26, 2013

Price: $9.99

Words: 17,600 (approximate)

Language: English

ISBN: 9781301001965

Contact for Advts.

Name: Capt Shekhar Gupta

Email: Csg.alfa@gmail.com

M: +919977513452